M000028858

DIVERSITY AND EXCLUSION:
CONFRONTING THE CAMPUS FREE SPEECH CRISIS

Copyright © 2021 by Lindsay Shepherd

All rights reserved.

ISBN: 978-0-9939195-7-2

Magna Carta

CONTENTS

INTRODUCTION

A number of people have encouraged me over the years to write a book detailing my experiences as a graduate student and teaching assistant at Wilfrid Laurier University, but I was resistant to it. Writing a book about myself and something I went through, as opposed to neutrally examining another subject, seemed too self-indulgent.

I vowed to instead write a book analyzing the ideology of diversity, equity, and inclusion in Canada, and how these weaselly concepts manifest themselves in academia, politics, media, and culture. As I was writing that book, I realized there was no way to avoid telling the story of the Laurier affair: so much of my knowledge and insight regarding diversity ideology, the suppression of open inquiry, and modern threats to free expression stemmed from my firsthand experiences at Laurier during the fall of 2017.

"Okay, fine," I said to myself, "I'll just briefly talk about Laurier in the introduction, before I get on with the rest of the book."

But there was no way the intricacies of the 2017–2018 Laurier controversy could be recounted in only a few pages.

This book before you is the one that needed to be written, for two reasons. Firstly, I have always enjoyed insider accounts of media-hyped events, and I'm guessing you and I share that quality. The second reason is more functional: documentation. Many have squinted at me when I tell them my name, remarking that it sounds somewhat familiar. After a moment they'll exclaim that I am "the TA who got fired for playing a Jordan Peterson video in class!" (Well, not quite). They will then add, "I don't really know the full story though, what actually ended up happening?"

This is that story.

PART I

CHAPTER 1

I didn't apply to graduate school because I was afraid of entering the full-time workforce, or because I was lacking something else to do. I also didn't care at all whether pursuing an MA would be some sort of "smart career move" that would look good on my resume and get me a higher salary.

In late 2016, when the end of my time as an undergraduate student was on the horizon, I applied to graduate school purely out of a desire for intellectual fulfillment and a love of reading, learning, and expanding my mind. Most of the potential career paths I was considering – teaching English to international students, applying to be a public relations officer with the Canadian Forces, or opening a small shop selling used clothing and goods – didn't require a graduate degree. But I figured I might eventually try to enter academia as a profession, because I saw the acquisition of knowledge and exploration of ideas as the most worthy pursuits in life.

I lived a humble existence in my bachelor suite in Burnaby, British Columbia, a 15-minute bus ride away from Simon Fraser University, where I was completing my BA in Communication and Political Science. I paid $735 a month in rent – utilities, internet, and cable included. There were raccoons living in my roof – I would hear their little feet scrambling around above my ceiling – but I was reluctant to tell my landlord about them. I didn't want the little raccoon family to be hurt or killed. My housemates, who lived in a separate suite, were somewhat heavy drinkers, so whenever they left beer cans and wine bottles in our recycling bin, I would promptly pluck them out and bike down to the bottle return depot for a bit of cash.

I didn't have an oven or dishwasher, and my fridge was usually bare, aside from a few bottles of near-empty hot sauces. But there was little cooking or cleaning to be done, as I was hardly ever home. I was either in class, writing my papers at the library, studying at the nearby 24-hour Tim Hortons, or working.

Throughout my undergraduate years, I juggled two to four part-time jobs at a time. I had been the manager of an artisan gelato shop; the events and promotions assistant for the SFU Recreation Centre; a program coordinator at a non-profit organization; and a childminder at a gym. I always downplayed how much I worked, since I didn't think people would believe me anyways. It was manageable, though: as the gelato shop manager, I could decide my own hours and work them around my classes, the SFU Recreation job was only five hours a week, the childcare facility job was only on Saturday and Sunday, and the program coordinator job was casual and you could sign up for your own shifts. My class readings were done on the bus to and from work and school. If I couldn't get a seat because the bus was too full, I would read standing up, my elbow hooked around a pole as I held my papers in one hand and a pink highlighter in the other.

I didn't get enough sleep at night, so if there happened to be a day where I had an hour or two of free time between classes, I would drift off in one of the comfy lounge chairs on campus. Sometimes, on my way home from working an evening shift, I would be lucky enough to get a seat on the bus where I could put my hood up and lean my head against the window for a half-hour snooze. I missed my stop countless times because of this, but I would sometimes miraculously wake up right at my stop and fly out the doors just before they closed shut. About once a week, I would drop into an on-campus yoga class, which I could attend for free as a recreation centre employee, and I'd spend the final five-minute savasana period making a mental checklist of all the things I needed to do that week (precisely what the yoga instructors tell you not to do during savasana). In one yoga class during a particularly busy week, I fell right asleep for that five minutes, my head resting on a cork yoga block.

I decided to apply only to graduate schools in Ontario, as I had never spent much time in the province. I had previously lived in both Montreal and Halifax – I moved to Halifax a month after graduating high school at 17 to attend Dalhousie University, but had a hard time securing part-time work to fund my studies. I transferred to Concordia University in Montreal, moving to a dingier neighbourhood in the borough of Verdun, also known as "Verdump." I waitressed at a Persian restaurant while taking courses in a bilingual policy studies program before deciding I missed my boyfriend at the time too much and moved back to BC.

Since my major at SFU was in Communication, it made sense to apply to graduate programs in the same field. People made fun of Communication Studies for being intellectually lightweight, or the degree of choice for scholarship football players, but I liked engaging in the analysis of media, technology, and modern Western culture. Though one of my friends, a geography student who had taken a course in Communication Studies, once told me that her impression of Communication students was that they are ambitious – but ambitious for things that don't matter. I agreed: it was always a bit off-putting to hear a classmate express that their dream job was being a social media engagement manager for Lululemon.

I applied to only two MA programs. The first was the MA Communication and New Media program at McMaster University in Hamilton. I cringed a bit when I applied: one of my professors had just happened to mention in class that "new media" was a terribly outdated term for "social media," explaining that no one in the field uses the term anymore. Next, I filled out my application to Wilfrid Laurier University. While looking at an alphabetical list of their MA programs, I saw a program titled "Cultural Analysis and Social Theory (CAST)" listed right after the Communication Studies program. It sounded intriguing – more complex and philosophical than Communication Studies. At the last minute, I applied for CAST instead of Communication Studies. With my writing samples submitted and references in order, all I could do for the next couple months was wait.

CHAPTER 2

In January 2017, I received my acceptance letters to both McMaster and Laurier. Each offered me a scholarship and a teaching assistantship.

I had a couple of weeks to decide which university to choose, and I was torn: McMaster was the more reputable university, but over the past couple months since submitting my application I had become hesitant to pursue Communication Studies at the graduate level. The themes commonly discussed in Communication Studies were getting stale: it seemed like every other day, I was listening to another student presentation about representation in the media. Many communication classes consisted of never-ending, circular discussions about how we need more ethnic, gender, and body size diversity on screen and behind the scenes. Even back in high school, our student presentations were about these things – especially when anorexia and bulimia were the topics *du jour* and everyone was exhausting the subject of how women's bodies are portrayed on runways and magazine covers and in advertisements.

Not to mention, at McMaster there was the ordeal of the program's title: could I really trust a degree program using the term "new media" to be cutting-edge?

"Oh Lindsay, choose McMaster," my grandma told me. "I looked online, and it's quite highly-ranked, whereas Wilfrid Laurier… it's a more, you know, middle-of-the-pack kind of place."

I was conscious of the disparity in university prestige, yet something was drawing me to Laurier. I didn't have any particular reason why: I just had a good feeling about it. Without having ever visited either university, I got the feeling that Laurier was the underdog: an up-and-coming and underrated place. And while there was a heavy emphasis on the name of your school in American culture, in Canada there was no Ivy League, so it seemed – to me, at least – the name of your school mattered less here.

There was something, though, that gave me pause about Laurier: a month prior to receiving my acceptance letter, the university had been in the news over a controversy involving the Wilfrid Laurier University Graduate Students' Association (GSA). The manager of the on-campus Veritas Café, a social enterprise operated by the GSA, posted a humorous job ad on Facebook that said "I need a new slave (full-time staff member) to boss around (mentor) at Veritas Café!" along with other light-hearted digs such as "Food safety certificate would help your cause too (we try not to kill our customers)" and "Cash handling is part of the job (but mostly debit and credit these days! Ugh! Damn fees)."[1]

Despite operating Veritas Café for nearly five years, manager Sandor Dosman's contract was promptly terminated, with Dosman's job ad (specifically his use of the word "slave") cited as the only reason for termination. The president of the GSA at the time hoped his firing could start "a larger conversation about tolerance and inclusivity on Laurier's campus."

Dosman's firing was ridiculous to me. When I worked at McDonald's as a teenager, many of my co-workers put "McSlave" and variations thereof as their job title on Facebook. I signed an online petition created by two Laurier students advocating for Dosman to get his job back. But, I figured, this was a total one-off situation, and it shouldn't affect my decision of whether or not to choose Laurier.

I declined McMaster's offer of admission, and accepted Laurier's.

*

After securing my future at grad school, I began to view myself as a more serious student. I was producing top-notch work and getting the best grades of my undergraduate career. That summer, I had a professor reach out to me and tell me I should apply to graduate school, and that he would gladly supply a reference – I pleasantly replied that I was two steps ahead of him. The final semester of my undergraduate degree was May–

August 2017, and then I would have a two-week break before moving to Waterloo and starting at Laurier in September.

That summer, I took on a new part-time job at a high-end juice shop that served $11-$12 single-serving bottles of organic cold-pressed juices and nut milks. The store received barely any business (they later ended up shuttering their stores in Vancouver), so I spent my shifts surfing through the modules of my online classes on the store iPad while I listened to jazz and drank day-old Brazilian Java (a nut milk blend of almonds, brazil nuts, cold brew coffee, dates, salt, vanilla, cinnamon and reishi mushroom). *Being paid to study*, I thought to myself as I sipped my drink. *I've really rigged the system!* Because there were barely any customers, the cashout, sweeping, and mopping at the end of the day only took 15 minutes or so. I would then pack up the unsold quinoa salad bowls and my boyfriend and I would eat them at either Kitsilano Beach or at a park in Yaletown, depending on which location I had been working at that day.

On a few occasions, the company was desperate for production workers, so I filled in a couple times at their factory warehouse, which was a very different experience. Rather than studying, drinking juice, and greeting the rare customer, I was sweating in a hot concrete warehouse; methodically and repetitively sticking labels on bottles, filling them up with juice, securing the bottle caps, and scrubbing the juicing equipment clean.

My second part-time job that summer was working as an editorial assistant for the Canadian Journal of Development Studies, where I edited peer-reviewed articles for spelling, grammar, punctuation, citation style, and the like – work I very much enjoyed, despite the eye strain caused by hours of squinting at a bright white screen, meticulously checking the placement of quotation marks and commas.

In the weeks leading up to my departure to Ontario, I made sure all of my affairs were in order: I gave my two weeks' notice to my bosses, donated boxes of clothing and kitchenware I wasn't taking with me, and listed my furniture on Craigslist. The night before my flight, various individuals – mostly other students – came to take away my coffee table, mattress, bed frame, and bookcases in exchange for $40 or $50 apiece. I cleaned until four in the morning and was out the door a couple hours later to catch my one-way flight to Waterloo.

CHAPTER 3

I quickly settled into my basement suite in Waterloo, right across from an elementary school surrounded by a grassy field and a network of trails that traversed the forests. I would often go running through the trails and see bunnies nibbling in the bush. The grass field was almost always empty, so I would use it to do squats, lunges, and push-ups in the open air. From the first day I arrived in Waterloo, it had struck me as the perfect place to raise a family – I envisioned a future me pushing a stroller down these peaceful sidewalks, taking my children out for an afternoon at the park. Alas, starting a family seemed so far off.

A few days before classes were set to begin, I took the bus to the Laurier campus to attend the MA Cultural Analysis and Social Theory (CAST) graduate orientation.

I went early to do a tour of the campus for the first time. There wasn't any particularly stunning architecture or any notable sights, or hip, high quality cafés, but Laurier was a pleasant place, I thought. The small campus could be best described as generic, but in a nice, comfortable kind of way. Most of the female students I passed by were dressed in a de facto uniform of Birkenstocks, black leggings, and a Laurier-branded hoodie.

I made my way over to the classroom where the MA CAST program coordinator, professor Herbert Pimlott, was sitting on a table at the front of the room with his arms crossed. I exchanged a few smiles with my soon-to-be classmates before taking my seat.

Pimlott introduced himself as an "accidental academic" – someone who hadn't aspired to go into academia but had ended up there. I could detect the faintest British accent: he was originally from the UK, where he had done his PhD at Goldsmiths College. He wore his shoulder-length blonde hair tied back in a ponytail.

Pimlott laid out the two streams you could take in the MA program – the course-based route or the major research paper (MRP) route. Both streams would result in the completion of an MA in 12 months, but the course-based program involved year-round coursework only, whereas the research paper stream was comprised of coursework from September to April, while May to August would be spent writing a 50-70 page paper under the guidance of a supervisor and a second advisor. I declared the MRP route: I wanted the experience and accomplishment of completing a capstone project. The MRP wasn't quite a thesis – master's theses would be 10-30 pages longer – but a master's thesis-stream program would typically take two years, and in this program I could be done in one year and still emerge with a major written work.

"Alright, now why don't we go around the room and you can introduce yourselves," said Pimlott. "You can say your name, where you finished your undergraduate degree, and what your potential research interest is for this MA program."

My first colleague provided their introduction, announcing they used "they/them" pronouns, and showed off a tattoo they had, which, if I recall correctly, was the roman numeral "XI" to represent Karl Marx's Eleventh Thesis on Feuerbach: "Philosophers have hitherto only interpreted the world in various ways; the point is to change it." My colleague explained that this quote, to them, meant that scholars have a duty to undertake real-world activism.

My turn came around: my research interest was the consolidation of cinema exhibitors in Canada, and how that might impact the availability of independent films. Cineplex, the top theatre exhibitor in Canada, was buying up many theatres across the country as many small, local cinemas were closing down due to the popularity of home streaming services like Netflix. My research interest at that time was to study whether communities were seeing more action-thriller blockbusters rather than lower-budget independent or foreign films when Cineplex took over the theatres by studying archives of movie theatre offerings.

As my other colleagues introduced themselves, discussing their interests in the areas of Islamophobia, homosexuality, queer studies, indigenous studies, Marxism, and feminism, my heart sank. The majority of my cohort was consumed by identity issues. I had encountered these types of people in my undergraduate years, and usually found them to be rather self-righteous and too eager to set up simplistic dichotomies of the oppressor and the oppressed.

A scary thought flickered in my mind: did I make a mistake in picking this program? I tried to shake the idea out of my head.

Should I have just applied to the MA Communication Studies program at Laurier instead? No, it wouldn't have mattered: I had been included in an email thread with the MA Communication Studies students, as I was going to be a TA in their department, and it seemed from their personal introductions that they were just as consumed with identity-related subjects as the CAST students. "I am interested in intersectional feminism, social justice, and sustainable technology" one of them had written in the email thread. "Where my interests lie is between building/identifying praxis/space between communities and academies (particularly that of liminal spaces) using gender, feminist, and queer theories and methodologies," another had said.

Even though I reckoned my colleagues and I had worldviews that were quite different, I still joined in whenever someone suggested we grab coffee and catch up after class. Talking about culture, philosophy, and politics with my colleagues at a campus coffee shop was how I had envisioned graduate school life.

I attended another orientation event in the first week of school, this time for all graduate students, university-wide. But I didn't stay for the whole production – too many of the workshops were about mental health. They were hammering us with the message that graduate school is going to be a really tough time and a lot of students end up suffering from depression and anxiety, but everything is going to be okay and if you need help you can talk to a counsellor on campus. There was nothing wrong with that message per se, but it seemed like these people were eager to pathologize us as anxious and stressed, and they had a certain infantilizing tone of voice that made me feel like I was at some kind of summer camp for kids with problems.

Finally, the last orientation session I attended was my TA orientation. I was placed as a TA for Communication Studies 101 – Canadian Communication in Context.

My supervisor, Nathan Rambukkana, explained the assignments we'd be marking throughout the year and walked us through the anti-plagiarism protocol. Rambukkana then sent us some sample lesson plans from past years, telling us we could use them if we wanted to, but that we could approach much of the teaching as we saw fit. Each class would generally open with a discussion period, where TAs would draw on the weekly reading-related discussion questions that students would post online, and then we would move on to an interactive lesson on that week's language-related topic, such as punctuation, style and language, or grammar. I was happy that Rambukkana was letting us approach our tutorials with our own style – he wasn't micromanaging us. For me, it was a dream come true to be a TA: it was one of the main reasons I had wanted to go to graduate school. I had been observing my own TAs for years; mentally recording what I liked and disliked about their teaching strategies. In late 2014, one of my TAs for an undergraduate Communication Studies course sparked a class discussion with the hottest news item that week: the Dalhousie Dentistry scandal. A private Facebook group consisting of several male dentistry students had its written contents leaked to the public, and the men were reprimanded at school for having discussed which of the female students in their department they would "hate fuck" and joking about having sex with unconscious women, along with other remarks that were widely condemned as misogynistic. Our TA opened the class by bringing up the scandal, and one of my classmates said, with a dismissive laugh, "I haven't heard anything about this, I'm American."

The TA was not impressed. "If you're not following the news, then maybe you shouldn't be in a Communication program," he deadpanned. I liked that: he had standards and expectations of his students. I vowed to be the same kind of TA.

*

It was a hot September in Waterloo. My grandma told me over the phone that Ontario leaves are beautiful in the fall, but I barely noticed the change of colour: throughout those weeks, I spent my days reading at the library, only really venturing out to go to class, refill my travel mug with coffee, or work out at the gym. In the evenings, I sat at the IKEA desk in my room, eating lentil stew and preparing my teaching materials by lamplight. On weekends, I would write my papers and finish assignments at the nearby Starbucks, for a change of scenery.

Although we were told at the graduate orientation that we'd all be riddled with anxiety and depression throughout our studies, I was finding graduate school suspiciously manageable. I had enough time to sleep eight hours a night and exercise four to five days a week. I loved working as a TA – it came naturally to me to stand up in front of that classroom and present in a manner that engaged my students – and I got the sense that my students liked me.

My graduate classes were not hard: I don't think I could even say they were more challenging than my second- or third-year undergraduate courses. I consulted with my friend from high school, Sophie, who went off to do a 12-month research paper stream MA at the same time I did, but in Newfoundland.

"Are you finding graduate school to be... dare I say... easy?" I texted her.

"Yes, totally. I thought it would be so much harder," she replied.

Of course, the easy time I was having was partially due to being an untethered individual – I didn't have any other responsibilities other than to work as a TA, complete my coursework, and compile preliminary research for my MRP. I had the luxury of spending all day on campus. That was how I had learned to succeed in university as an undergraduate: plop myself down at the library and not leave until it was dark. If I completed my main tasks for the day earlier than expected, I would stay in my seat and get a head start on something else before going home. When I was on my computer in a public space, I wouldn't get distracted by frivolous activities like online shopping or silly videos – I would be too embarrassed if anyone were to walk by my screen and see that I was slacking off. One of my favourite memories from my undergraduate years was sitting in a class titled "Global Problems and the Culture of Capitalism" and watching the girl in front of me shopping on Amazon as she nodded her head to the instructor's lecture.

*

Soon enough, an autumn chill descended upon Waterloo, and the sun was setting in the late afternoon.

Throughout those first months of graduate school, though I had an established routine, good grades, and high morale at my teaching assistantship, I couldn't deny that I was feeling a bit lost. My graduate class readings had titles like "The Camp as Biopolitical Paradigm of the Modern," "Dialectics of Colonial Sovereignty," and "The Future Birth of the Affective Fact: The Political Ontology of Threat." These titles might sound compelling at first, but once you read the chapters or papers, you are left wondering what you even learned, as there seemed to be no original point or argument. I had to be frank with myself: not only did I find my classes to be easy, but I found that they were in no way advancing me intellectually. I had a hard time coming to terms with that – I had always abhorred when people mocked liberal arts students for having a worthless education that would only lead them to working as a barista. Firstly, because I truly valued the liberal arts and humanities, and secondly, because I didn't see baristas as people to be looked down upon.

I couldn't help but feel alienated by the endless references to Karl Marx, Gilles Deleuze, Jacques Derrida, Jacques Lacan, Judith Butler, and above all, Michel Foucault, who I found barely had any interesting ideas at all. Sometimes, when people asked me, "A degree in Cultural Analysis and Social Theory? What's that?" I would flatly answer, "Foucault worship." I once expressed in class how disillusioned I felt with the amount of time we devoted to Foucault, and said I didn't feel like anything he said was particularly well-expressed. Announcing such a point of view is difficult, as one can easily come off as outright anti-intellectual. What gives me the right to be criticizing Michel Foucault, the most-cited scholar in the humanities? But to my surprise, many of my classmates vocally agreed with me, at which point it came to my attention that almost everyone in my MA cohort was either disenchanted with or confused by our program. (In my personal journal, I wrote in an October 22, 2017 entry, "No one seems to know what they're doing here.") I would also later learn that the MA CAST program had been on the chopping block a few years prior, but was somehow managing to stay alive.

The Cultural Analysis and Social Theory program also had a heavy emphasis on "biopolitics," which, in my view, was crock. "Biopolitical theory" was synonymous with nothingness. The Oxford bibliography entry on the subject will tell you:[2]

> *"Biopolitics" is a term that refers to the intersection and mutual incorporation of life and politics. In literal terms, it signifies a form of politics that deals with life (Greek: bios). Yet if we begin from this basic definition, a series of questions immediately arises: What is life? What is politics? What is the precise nature of the relation between these two things? Do all forms of politics relate to life? Different answers exist to these questions.*

My department was home to a working group on biopolitics, and one of the elective courses I could have taken (but most certainly did not) was

"Biopolitical Theory," which was a whole course in Foucault worship, with a sprinkling of Donna Haraway and Giorgio Agamben. Studying "biopolitics" was a way of pretending to study an interdisciplinary meld of sociology, ethics, government, and medicine, when really it was the study of nothing. The biopolitics acolytes deployed a specialized, obscure language that made it seem like they were doing something so distinguished that a layperson just could simply not understand it, when really there was nothing substantive about what they were saying. The nothingness of their endeavour was cloaked with fancy terms like "necropolitics," "subjectivity," and "governmentality."

My program didn't have a proper research methods class either – we had an "Approaches to Cultural Analysis" class that taught post-structuralism, postcolonial thought, "decolonization and emancipatory methodologies," and "feminist epistemology." In the course syllabus, the professor wrote that she wanted us to appreciate the scholars that "debunk, disrupt, and dislocate the hegemonic notion of Modernity, the power-knowledge relations that stem from it, and complicate the (Western-white-male) subjectivity that comes with it." In these types of classes, as long as the root argument of your papers was "colonialism = bad" and "patriarchy = bad," you could ace all of your assignments.

I was very much opposed to credentialism, but I dealt with my MA program disillusionment by telling myself that even if I didn't gain any knowledge from my program, at least I'd have the degree. Getting through with good grades wouldn't be a problem: I was already getting high marks. All you had to do was name-drop the right scholars in your presentations and write your "reading reflection papers" with contemporary academic jargon. It upset me to approach my graduate studies in this manner – as an end-goal rather than an enriching intellectual experience – but it was the only way I could justify remaining enrolled.

In search of solace, I found myself one day sitting in the corner of a Starbucks, resisting doing my readings, and instead typing phrases into the Google search bar like "Why is my grad program all about feminism, postmodernism, and Marx?" and "Feel like I'm not learning anything in arts grad school." A sparse number of articles that critiqued the presence of postmodernism, poststructuralism, intersectional feminism, and Marxism in academia popped up. It feels strange to say, but I had never come across such articles before. I had never sought them out. I considered the university to be the most important institution in the world, and regarded anyone who criticized arts and humanities programs to be a philistine. The only articles I had read that criticized the university discussed the institution's overreliance on underpaid, precarious sessional instructors and the "publish or perish" model that valued the quantity rather than quality of academic papers.

One online publication I came across in my search was called Areo. I found a title that read "The Woes of Academia,"[3] where author Malhar Mali wrote:

> ...your idea for an academic paper could be as banal, abstract, and ridiculous as possible but as long as one reader is interested, the project is acceptable. I'd imagine it's easy to find a reader in an academic environment where your professor is heavily invested in concepts such as reflections of gender and race while watching videos of people trying to dance like Beyoncé.

> Where these academic tendencies come from, I do not know. My best venture is that they're the bastardized versions of postmodern, critical race, feminist, and gender study theories, put forth by devout theorists thirsty to see power structures where they do not exist, eager to "deconstruct" realities meanwhile creating their own, and striving to create oppression when it's not evident. Obviously, Academia is still mired by the demon of Publish or Perish— academics have to churn out papers to be considered relevant but it's easy to see how "pursuing knowledge for the sake of knowledge" is perverted in the humanities and social sciences.

I later stumbled upon an almost two-hour long YouTube conversation between Dr. Jordan Peterson and Camille Paglia, where the pair discussed postmodernism in the academy. Perhaps I found the video through my search terms like "problems in universities today" or perhaps the YouTube algorithm suggested the video to me, I can't say for sure. I had only vaguely heard of Jordan Peterson. When I was visiting my mom's house one day, back as an undergraduate student, she had shown me an article in the newspaper about how a University of Toronto psychology professor was being shouted down at McMaster University by students who didn't like his views on gender pronouns or compelled speech. The students were using airhorns to drown him out.

"Isn't that just so wrong?" my mom asked, shaking her head. "It's censorship!"

"I guess?" I shrugged, turning back to whatever I had been doing before, and not giving it a second thought.

I did know who Camille Paglia was: I had watched an interview with her on the CBC in May 2017. I distinctly recall seeing a flash of horror in interviewer Wendy Mesley's eyes when Paglia said, in a discussion about sexual assault on college campuses, "If you go to a fraternity house party… and a young man says to you, would you like to go up to my room, I'm sorry ok, you are consenting to sex. He is right to think you have consented." I considered what Paglia said to be rape apologism, but I found her intriguing. I was always drawn to those who spoke with such confidence and could easily laugh off criticism.

In the exchange between Paglia and Peterson, they were dropping the names of theorists I was reading in my courses – Derrida, Foucault, Lacan, and the like – but instead of praising them, they were calling them "tricksters" and "intellectual midgets" who were looking everywhere for homophobia, racism, and sexism. "They are like high priests murmuring to each other," said Paglia. She mocked what she called the "fancy contorted jargon of the pseudo-leftists of academe, who are frauds. These people who managed to rise to the top… they are career people, they're corporate types… they love the institutional context, they know how to manipulate the bureaucracy which is totally invaded and usurped."

"These people are company players… They love to sit in endless committees, they love bureaucratic regulation and so on."

Peterson added, "The skeptical part of me thinks that postmodernism is an intellectual camouflage for the continuation of the kind of pathological Marxism that produced the Soviet Union, and it has no independent existence as an intellectual field whatsoever."

Peterson and Paglia were openly criticizing the same phenomena I was privately skeptical about. I too found these theories and theorists uninteresting, unoriginal, and unenlightening, but I felt like I had to like them, otherwise I had no place being at a university.

Peterson expressed, in regard to Michel Foucault, "I read Madness and Civilization and a couple of his other books, and I thought that they were painfully obvious." Paglia criticized Foucault for masquerading as a leftist; using academic jargon that was inaccessible to the real leftist working class.

Though I can't remember in precisely what order I watched the YouTube videos, I also came across another video that I found intriguing – this one from TVO, or TV Ontario, the province's publicly funded television station. The October 2016 episode "Genders, Rights, and Freedom of Speech" was premised on the controversy that had catapulted Jordan Peterson to international fame that year. Peterson had publicly voiced his concerns over Bill C-16, "An Act to amend the Canadian Human Rights Act and the Criminal Code," which would add "gender expression" and "gender identity" as protected grounds to the Canadian Human Rights Act. Peterson was concerned that Bill C-16 (which passed in 2017 and is now law in Canada) would compel Canadians to use words like "zie" and "zer" against their will, entrapping them in the language of radical leftist ideology.

The always-measured namesake host of TVO's The Agenda with Steve Paikin, Steve Paikin, asked Peterson to lay his case out as to why he takes issue with the legislation.

"Well fundamentally, there were two things that really bothered me… one was that I was being asked, as everyone is, to use a certain set of words that I think are the constructions of people who have a political ideology that I don't believe in and that I also regard as dangerous," Peterson replied.

"What are those words?" asked Paikin.

"Those are the made-up words that people now describe as gender-neutral. And so to me they're an attempt to control language and in a direction that isn't happening organically, it's not happening naturally, people aren't picking up these words in the typical way that new words are picked up, but by force and by fiat, and I would say by force because there's legislative power behind it. And I don't like these made-up words, 'zie' and 'zer' and that sort of thing."

"Ok what about – they're not all made-up words, quote unquote made-up words, for example, 'they' is one of them, to speak to an individual as 'they,'" Paikin pushed back.

"Yes, right, but we can't dispense with the distinction between singular and plural. I mean, I know that the advocates of that particular approach say that 'they' has been used forever as a singular and that's actually not correct. It's used as a singular in very exceptional circumstances."

I was scheduled to teach grammar in my Communication Studies 101 tutorials for the next two weeks, and this discussion seemed like it would be very instructive for my students: it was fascinating how a grammar and language-related debate was a hot topic on a TV panel show.

In the Grammar section of our class textbook, the Little Pearson Handbook, there was a section on "Sexist Pronouns:"[4]

> English does not have a neutral singular pronoun for a group of mixed genders or a person of an unknown gender... One strategy is to use *her or his* or *his and her*... Often you can avoid using *his or her* by changing the noun to the plural form.
>
> *All students must select their courses using the online registration system.*
>
> In some cases, however, using *his* or *her* is necessary.

In the previous section of our textbook, Style and Language, there was a subsection titled "Be inclusive about gender," which discussed the outmoded way of referring to both genders with only masculine nouns and pronouns, such as saying "mankind" instead of "humankind" or "Every employee must return his equipment at the end of his shift" when referring to both male and female employees. The book stated "biased masculine pronouns" should be replaced by them, they, or their. I agreed.

The TVO clip would complement this textbook content nicely and help my students see the real-life implications of seemingly uninteresting grammar rules. Imagine, pronouns were a cultural, societal, and legal issue of serious interest in our country!

I asked another TA what she was planning to teach in her grammar tutorial. She told me she and the other TAs had prepared a lesson based on examples of bad grammar in celebrity tweets. It struck me as a strange lesson, seeing as Twitter was built around the idea of a strict character limit, which meant commas, apostrophes, conjunctions, and other sentence components were often omitted for the sake of space. I wasn't going to teach my students about grammatically incorrect celebrity tweets. It was settled then: I would screen the short TVO clip of the grammar debate as part of my lesson.

I found another clip to complement the exchange between Peterson and Paikin, where Peterson and Professor of Transgender Studies Nicholas Matte argued about the human impact of pronouns. Matte said that misusing students' pronouns is violence, abuse, and hate speech, because trans students using alternate pronouns need their humanity and dignity to be recognized. Peterson strikes back, saying,

> ...*if our society comes to some sort of consensus over the next while about how we'll solve the pronoun problem, let's call it, and that becomes part of popular parlance and it seems to solve the problem properly without sacrificing the distinction between singular and plural and without requiring me to memorize an impossible list of an indefinite number of pronouns, then I would be willing to reconsider my position... there are things that are at stake in this discussion, despite its surface nature, that strike at the very heart of our civilization.*

I enjoyed panel discussions like this one, as I admired personalities from either side of the debate who could clearly and convincingly state their position. I was interested in hearing my students' insights on the video clips – I felt both Peterson and Matte had arguments that some might find convincing.

I didn't have any strong position myself. But I was about to learn that that was a problem.

CHAPTER 4

One of my fellow TAs asked me to cover for her class on November 1, 2017, so that evening I would be teaching three blocks of tutorials as opposed to my usual two. Now, if I had known that these three particular classes would be impacting the trajectory of my life, I would have tried to remember every painstaking detail from those three hours, and rushed to write down as much as I could as soon as I got home. But alas, I treated that day like any other day of teaching, and can only recall a general outline of the evening.

I greeted each class of 25 or so first-year Communication Studies students and took attendance. For the first portion of the class, we discussed the weekly readings and I answered student questions about the material before moving on to the language component of the class.

"What is grammar?" I asked the room of students.

I switched on my PowerPoint presentation to a slide that read:

Grammar:

SYNTAX (the arrangement of words & phrases to create well-formed sentences)

+

MORPHOLOGY (the forms of words).

For the next several slides, I went over some common grammatical errors, like the conflation of affect/effect; they're/their/there; your/you're; and its/it's. I made up sample sentences, read them aloud, and got my students to identify which word would be correct. This went on for the majority of the 50-minute class.

My eighth slide read "Current Issues in Grammar: Pronouns," and the ninth, "Their vs. His or Her." We talked about the textbook content that went over inclusive language, discussing how masculine pronouns and nouns are no longer accepted as the default in any written work. I asked my students what they thought about using "they" in the singular, and we discussed in what context we might already be using "they" in the singular without realizing it, such as when we are referring to someone whose gender we don't yet know.

It was at this point in my tutorial that I introduced the clip from The Agenda. We watched the clips I had selected. While there were generally always a few students in my tutorials tapping away on their phones and laptops and ignoring the class content, it seemed that for once, everyone was staring up at the large screen at the front of the room. When the clips had concluded, I turned to the class and asked for their thoughts, giving my students the opportunity to gain participation points by discussing whether they found Peterson and Matte to have made convincing cultural, grammatical, or linguistic arguments.

Whenever a student was strongly on one side, I would offer a counterpoint, which was always received with a nod of acknowledgment or a thoughtful murmur. Only in one of my classes did a student who sat at the back of the room make some sort of comment asking whether he could identify as a pixie stick or a unicorn. I stared at him blankly and flatly said "hm" before moving on to the next raised hand. It was the only comment of that nature from the three classes.

I then brought up how in English, we use gendered pronouns, but in the Persian language (which I had been studying formally for three years, as my boyfriend at the time was Iranian), pronouns were not gendered: he and she were both *ou,* or colloquially, *oon.* I relayed this example to my students and asked if they had any other examples from languages that they spoke. In each class, at least one student pointed out that language is constantly in flux, as we don't speak Shakespearean English anymore, and change was okay.

With that, I moved on to the "Fragments" section of my tutorial and talked about how to avoid fragmented sentences until the 50-minute time block concluded. After my final class that evening, I slid my notebooks and laptop into my backpack, switched off the lights, and headed to the bus stop. The classes went late: my last tutorial of the night ended at 9:50pm. I got home and ate lentil stew at my desk while I went over my readings for the next day and had a cup of hot Earl Grey tea before going to bed. Just like any other night.

*

The following week, I was sitting at a cubicle in a communal graduate student office when an email popped up from CS101 course professor Nathan Rambukkana. The last time I'd seen him in person was in late October for a group meeting to discuss the marking protocol of the annotated bibliography assignment. The title of the email said "Meeting to Discuss Concerns Tomorrow." Concerns? I cautiously clicked on the email.

> *Hi Lindsay,*
>
> *I'm wondering if you could come in for a meeting tomorrow (Wednesday the 8th) at 2:30 in my office (DAWB 3-136). There have been some concerns over some of the content of your tutorials and we should meet to discuss them and how to move forward. As the head of your program, Dr. Pimlott will also attend the meeting and I have also asked a member of the Diversity and Equity Office to be there as well.*
>
> *Please let me know if this timing is possible.*
>
> *All best,*
>
> *Nathan*

His email signature read: *"We have to be there at the birth of ideas, the bursting outward of their force: not in books expressing them, but in events manifesting this force, in struggles carried on around ideas, for or against them."* — Michel Foucault

I was stunned. What kind of email was this? He wouldn't even say what I had done wrong, or what the concerns were. But because this was coming after I had taught my class on grammar, I could only deduce that this was about the TVO clip. Why couldn't Rambukkana just describe over email what the problem was, and how to fix it? It was always fishy when people wouldn't put anything in writing.

As I read the email over and over again, exclamation marks were going off in my head – why would my MA program coordinator, Herbert Pimlott, have to be there? Was my standing as an MA student at risk?

And I was not the type who needed intervention from a Diversity and Equity Office! I was a quiet, sensitive person who minded my own business!

A thought occurred to me: I should indeed attend the meeting, at the time suggested, but secretly record it – just in case. The vagueness of the email was just too suspicious: "concerns" about "some of the content?" We need to discuss how to "move forward?" And these alleged "concerns" were such a serious matter that it required the intervention of my supervising professor, my graduate program coordinator, and some sort of diversity enforcer?

I called my mom and read her the email, asking for her opinion.

"You should record the meeting," she said.

"That's exactly what I was thinking," I replied.

*

I had some prior experience dabbling in controversy at school, even if I hadn't realized at the time I was apparently being so provocative.

One day, in my Grade 10 drama class, we were told to partner up for an exercise and given a very short script. The exercise was to exchange the word "Yes" a half-dozen times each, back and forth, but with contextual cues to make a descriptive scenario based on the script, which we would present to the class.

"I have an idea," I said to my scene partner. "Let's pretend we're smoking pot." I imitated holding a joint, and nodded my head slowly as I said "Yes," relaxing my eyelids as if I were stoned. I had never smoked pot before and had been dreadfully afraid of drugs ever since seeing the movie *Thirteen*; I was only imitating the media depictions I had seen of marijuana smokers.

My partner and I practiced our skit, reclining next to one another. We exchanged the word "Yes," varying the intonation to be thoughtful, mellow, and excited, as we held our thumb and index fingers together and pretended to take little puffs.

When it was time to present, my partner and I took our spots in front of our class, leaned back beside each other and started puffing.

"Yes," I said, in a typical stoner-dude voice.

"Yes," my partner said with the same inflection.

"Stop!" the voice of our drama teacher reverberated from the back of the room, interrupting our skit. My partner and I looked at each other, scared.

"This is not appropriate," the teacher shook his head. "You two, come here, and everyone gather round. I need everyone to listen up."

"This kind of presentation is not what we do in this class," the teacher said sternly. He preached to the whole class about how our presentation was not acceptable, as we did not handle the topic of drugs with sensitivity and care.

We didn't receive any punishment, other than being made to redo our skit with a new premise and being spoken to as if we had done something abhorrent and borderline criminal. After the talking-to, my partner scowled at me. I don't know what perception I had of political correctness in the tenth grade, but I knew instinctively that this teacher was being a pearl-clutcher. Drama class was supposed to be about artistic expression, creative exploration, and the pushing of boundaries: our teacher seemed way too uptight to be teaching this class.

Another time, in Grade 11, on my daily commute to school one morning, I was handed a little magazine from the Jehovah's Witnesses while passing through a public transit station. While waiting for my bus, I sat on a bench and took out some scissors from my pencil case. I cut out every picture of Jesus Christ in the magazine, as well as every heading that referenced the name "Jesus Christ," such as "What does Jesus Christ mean to you?" I glued the cut-outs to a piece of paper to make a collage. The final result was a pastel-tone collage of various shapes and sizes of Jesus images, with phrases about Jesus Christ pasted here and there. I thought it was actually quite subversively artistic. I was very interested in atheism at the time, and enjoyed watching clips of talk shows with Christopher Hitchens and Bill Maher. I have always hated vacuous discussions about "celebrity crushes," but if I did have a celebrity crush in my teenage years, it would have been Bill Maher.

Just to have a bit of fun, I made two photocopies of the poster once I got to school and posted them up on the wall. My Burnaby high school by no means had a large Christian population, but the handful of Hispanic Catholic students found out I made the poster and got very, very angry. They were connected to gang activity, and called on the local Burnaby gang members to come to the school and fight me. Two Colombian girls in my grade cornered me near the lockers, and one of them shoved me at the shoulders and ordered me not to mock or make fun of her religion. The next day at school, about six or seven of the Hispanic gang members were waiting for me in the hallway, but fortunately did not approach me: they just hollered at me as I walked by that I was a "skinny white bitch." Notably, most of them were stubby and overweight. I yelled back, "Thank you!" Once the school became aware of the gang's presence, they called me and my mother into the office, and I was sent home for the rest of the day for "my own safety."

But by showing the TVO clip in my CS101 class, I was not trying to be the rabble-rouser I had been in Grade 11 – I genuinely found it to be a levelled, informative, and topical discussion.

*

Less than 24 hours after receiving Rambukkana's email, I was in his office, right at 2:30pm. He was seated across from me, with a notebook and pen in his hands. Herbert Pimlott was on my left, twiddling his thumbs and avoiding eye contact, and Acting Manager of Gendered Violence and Sexual Assault Prevention Adria Joel was on my right, looking at me sternly.

We all greeted one another.

"Do you know why you're here today?" Rambukkana asked me as I took a seat.

"The only thing I can possibly think of is that I played a TVO clip featuring Dr. Jordan Peterson in my tutorial," I answered. "Also, do you mind if I take notes?" I asked, reaching for my laptop.

"Yes, that's right," Rambukkana said approvingly, "And no, not at all, go ahead."

I opened my MacBook Air, clicked on the Photobooth app, and launched the audio and video recording. The camera was facing my torso, only filming my sweater. I quickly opened a blank Word document on top of the Photobooth app. I tilted my screen toward me so neither Pimlott or Joel could see the green light near the built-in webcam that indicated recording was in progress.

From here, I present you with the full transcript of the meeting, captured in the recording.[5]

> Rambukkana: Do you see why that might have been seen as problematic by some of the students. Maybe even threatening?
>
> Shepherd: I don't see how someone would rationally think it was threatening. I could see how it might challenge their existing ideas, but for me, that's the spirit of the university – challenging ideas that you already have. I don't know who this came from, I would be interested to see the original complaint, or complaints, because I don't have any context as to what exactly their problem was.
>
> Pimlott: Sorry to interrupt, but can I just ask Lindsay to maybe just provide us with the full thing? Sorry I'd just like to hear the whole – what took place. So if you could just give us the whole story. And then, sorry, but I feel that because I'm just sitting in.
>
> Shepherd: Yep, okay, so we have to teach about grammar. In the Pearson book, there was a section about pronouns, and using gendered language. So, I wanted to make it more engaging, so what I did, we were

33

talking about using "they" as a singular. And we were also talking about "his and hers" and how to construct sentences with that. And then, to contextualize it, I brought up a YouTube debate, so a debate with both sides, Jordan Peterson's side, and this fellow named Nicholas Matte, who is also a prof at U of T.

Rambukkana: Do you have the name of the video?

Shepherd: It was from The Agenda with Steve Paikin. It was a YouTube debate, it was one hour long, but I showed about five minutes. And I mean, the students were very interested, I could tell, all their eyes were on the screen. After, when we had a debate, there were people of all opinions. From what I could see, it was a very friendly debate. Obviously, this person who had an issue did not express it to me, they just went straight to whoever, I don't really know what happened.

Rambukkana: Okay, so just for some additional context, you came from U of T, is that right?

Shepherd: No. From SFU.

Rambukkana: Oh. From SFU? Okay, so you weren't one of Jordan Peterson's students or anything like that.

Shepherd: No.

Rambukkana: Just to give you some context about Jordan Peterson, he is a figure that is basically highly involved with the alt-right.

At this point, I furrowed my brow and lightly shook my head.

Rambukkana: He – yes – the website Rebel Media, which is an alt-right website, has been involved in raising multiple hundreds of thousands of dollars for his research. About a week and a half ago, he gave a lecture in which he identified student protesters by posting their social media accounts so people would bully and threaten them online. He lectures about basically critiquing feminism, critiquing trans rights, critiquing white supremacy – er, not critiquing –

Shepherd: I mean, I'm familiar, I follow him. But, the thing is, can you shield people from those ideas? Am I supposed to comfort them and make sure that they are insulated away from this? Is that what the point of this is? Because to me that is so against what a university is about. So against it. I was not taking sides, I was presenting both arguments.

Rambukkana: So the thing is about this, if you're presenting something like this, you have to think about the kind of teaching climate that you're creating. These arguments are counter to the Canadian Human Rights Code, and I know you talked about C-16. Ever since this passed, it is discriminatory to be targeting someone due to their gender identity or gender expression. So bringing something like

that up in class, not critically, and I
understand that you're trying to -

It dawned on me exactly what he was suggesting: Criticizing or
questioning Bill C-16 was in violation of Bill C-16. Not only that, but
apparently discussing the grammar of pronouns was counter to the
Canadian Human Rights Code.

Shepherd: It was critical. I introduced it
critically.

Rambukkana: How so?

Shepherd: Like I said, it was in the
spirit of debate.

Rambukkana: Okay, "in the spirit of
debate" is slightly different than "This
is a problematic idea that maybe we want
to unpack."

Shepherd: But that's taking sides.

Rambukkana: Yes.

Shepherd: But that's taking sides for me
to be like "Oh look at this guy.
Everything that comes out his mouth is BS
but we're gonna watch anyway."

Rambukkana: Okay. So, I understand the
position that you're coming from and your
positionality, but the reality is, that it
has created a toxic climate for some of
the students. You know, it's great that-

Shepherd: How many? Who? How many? One?

Rambukkana: May I speak?

Shepherd: I have no concept of how many
people complained, what their complaint
was. You haven't shown me the complaint.

At this point, I tear up. I was so dreadfully confused as to why I was
being told complaints were made against me, but I wasn't allowed to
know how many people complained, or what the complaints said. I
wanted to see what the complainant had written. I wanted proof.

Rambukkana: Yes I understand that this is
upsetting, but there is also
confidentiality matters.

Shepherd: The number of people is
confidential?

Rambukkana: Yes.

Shepherd: Okay.

Rambukkana: It's one or multiple students
who have come forward saying that this is
something that they were concerned about
and that it made them uncomfortable. If
this is for example, a trans student, this
is basically debating whether or not a
trans student should have rights within
one of their classes. That's not something
that is really acceptable in the context
of the kind of learning environment that
we're trying to create. It would be the
equivalent of debating whether or not a
student of colour should have rights, or
should be allowed to be married. Do you
see how this is not something that is
intellectually neutral, that is up for
debate? I mean, this is the Charter of
Rights and Freedoms.

Shepherd: But it is up for debate.

Rambukkana: You're perfectly welcome to your own opinions, but when you're bringing it into the context of the classroom, that can become problematic, and that creates an unsafe learning environment for students.

Shepherd: But when they leave the university, they're going to be exposed to these ideas. So I don't see how I'm doing a disservice to the class by exposing them to ideas that are really out there. I'm sorry I'm crying, I'm stressed out, because this to me is so wrong. So wrong.

Joel: Can we mention the Gendered and Sexual Violence Policy?

Rambukkana: Yeah, please.

Joel: So under that, gendered violence doesn't just include sexual violence, but it also includes targeting folks based on gender, so that includes transphobia, biphobia, homophobia. All those sorts of things are protected under the policy, and so those are things that Laurier has upheld as values as well as the Ontario Human Rights Code. So those are things that we're responsible for not impacting our students in that way, and not spreading transphobia.

Shepherd: Okay, so, what I have a problem with, is that I didn't target anybody, who did I target?

Joel: Trans folks.

Shepherd: How? By telling them ideas that
are really out there? By telling them
that? By telling them? Really?

Rambukkana: It's not just telling them, in
legitimizing this as a valid perspective,
as this is another valid perspective-

Shepherd: In a university, all
perspectives are valid.

Rambukkana: That's not necessarily true,
Lindsay.

Shepherd: Well, this is something that's
being debated in current society, and I
don't feel the need to shield people from
what's going on in society.

Rambukkana: Okay.

Shepherd: To imagine that this is
happening in a university? It's just bad.
Bad.

Rambukkana: Okay, so just to give you a
context, also within all of this that is
happening, Laurier is being blanketed with
white supremacist posters currently.

I furrowed my brow again, as I had not seen one single "white
supremacist poster" on the Laurier campus since September, and I was
exactly the kind of person who went out of my way to stop in the
hallways to check out the latest posters.

Rambukkana: There is another debate in
society, which is whether or not North
America should be a set of white
nationalist states and that they should be
ethnically cleansed of other people. That

is also a current debate in society. Would you show something in your tutorial that you had, you know, white supremacists and non-white supremacists debating whether or not other people should live in North America. Is that something that you would show?

Shepherd: If that was related to the content of the week and we were talking about right-wing speech bubbles, maybe.

Rambukkana: Okay.

Shepherd: And it depends on the content, if there are really ideas that are existing out there like that, then I mean - Look, the thing is, I don't see what's transphobic about showing a video of Jordan Peterson. He's a real person. He's out there!

Rambukkana: He is a real person. But he is a real person who has engaged in targeting of trans students, basically doxxing them, if you know the term, giving out their personal information, so that they'll be attacked, harassed, so that death threats will find them.

This was simply not true.

Rambukkana: This is something that he has done to his own students, that he has done to other students, and this is something that the students are aware of. So this is basically like playing - not to kind of do the thing where everything is compared to Hitler - but this is like neutrally playing a speech by Hitler or Milo

Yiannopoulos from Gamergate. This is the kind of thing that departmentally, in terms of critical communication studies, and in terms of the course and what we're trying to do, is diametrically opposed to everything that we've been talking about in the lectures. Was this one of the reasons that you wanted to do this? As a reaction to the lecture content?

Shepherd: No, we were talking about gendered language. I was asking them to structure sentences using "they" or using "his or her" and then we talked about the societal context of it.

Rambukkana: Okay.

Shepherd: So I don't get why I'm being seen as transphobic, by virtue, by proxy, of me just saying, just exposing people to an idea. I don't get how that label is attached to me, I really don't.

Rambukkana: It's more about the effect, than the intention. Obviously, that wasn't your intention, but nevertheless, it disturbed and upset students enough–

Shepherd: So everything is about those students who are disturbed? Everything is catered to them?

Rambukkana, who had been taking notes, began furiously scribbling.

Rambukkana: Lindsay–

Pimlott: Can I offer a different perspective?

Rambukkana: Yeah.

Pimlott: Was this a tutorial based on looking at grammar?

Shepherd: Mhm.

Pimlott: And it was focused on the use of pronouns and the use of grammar?

Shepherd: Mhm.

Pimlott: Is grammar not something that's not really subject to debate?

Shepherd: They, and his and her? It's a huge debate right now: can we use "they" in the singular?

Pimlott: But you do know, that "they" has actually been used in the singular, it's grammatically –

Shepherd: Yeah, and that was in the video I showed to the class, and a point I made. What's kind of funny, is I disagree with Jordan Peterson. I disagree. But you guys seem to think that I'm pro-Jordan Peterson or something.

At that time, I was on the fence about Jordan Peterson, or perhaps in denial about how much his words resonated with me.

Rambukkana: Well, from the –

Pimlott: Sorry, do you mind If I...?

Rambukkana: Sorry, yeah, go ahead.

Pimlott: I'm here for a different reason, just as the MA CAST coordinator. My issue with Jordan Peterson, I'm gonna come at it from a different angle, is that as an academic and scholar in this institution, or any institution in which - My research is subject to peer review. You know what peer review is, right?

Shepherd: Mhm.

A condescending question to ask a graduate student, no?

Pimlott: So, regardless of what I believe, if I'm to be published in scholarly journals, my research has to be demonstrated to be able to be reproduced in the methods and theories that are used to reproduce it. I might believe X, but my academic freedom, as I understand it, does not just give me the freedom to spout off. If I'm tenured and they can't fire me, I mean there's the case of Charles Murray, he used to do this about race at Western, wasn't it Western? Yeah.

Pimlott meant J. Philippe Rushton, the now-deceased Western University professor who studied race and intelligence and published what is deemed to be dubious research. Charles Murray, who is still alive, is a social scientist who co-authored The Bell Curve, a book that discusses the role human intelligence plays in the prediction of life outcomes.

Pimlott: He published stuff by publishing companies that didn't do peer review because they wanted what he had. So what he was actually teaching his students were ideas that were not substantiated by methods and theories that could not be reproduced in an academic and analytical way, that other people reproduce and get

43

the same results. He had already
predetermined the outcome. It's much the
way a lot of these right-wing think tanks,
like the Fraser Institute, their form of
research can't be done in traditional
academic journals because they've already
predetermined the outcome. For myself,
regardless of what I believe, I will not
teach anything in any of my classes if it
is not something that is substantiated by
evidence that can be reproduced according
to peer review. I might tell students that
I might believe X, I have no expectations
that they will reproduce anything that I
think because I don't expect them to. I
say I believe X because of what I've read.
But for me, as I teach the students in the
second year Comm Studies theory course,
is, I know it's a bit simplistic, opinion
minus evidence equals prejudice. In the
case of Jordan Peterson, and I'm not super
well-versed, but I have done reading and
looking at – none of his contentions about
the Human Rights Code, the fact that
people can be jailed – I mean, you
probably believe – if you follow him you
would know that he claims you could be
jailed, when C-16 was being discussed. He
was claiming you could be jailed, if you
misgendered, used the wrong pronoun for
someone. What struck me was that none of
what he proclaimed, and sometimes how he
proclaims it, I think he tries to act like
he doesn't yet know – is done in ways that
are academically suspect, to say the
least. From what I've read in research,
which is again, I'm not as extensive on
researching him. He does not have the
substantial academic evidence to be a
credible person. It's like some of the

climate change deniers that are given a
50/50 chance with meteorologists.
Scientists never proclaim 100%, because
the scientific method cannot demonstrate –
you know no scientist says "this is 100%
certain" because that's the nature of
scientific inquiry, just like social
scientific inquiry. In the same way
though, meteorologists do not teach in
first year geology or meteorological
classes that there is a debate, even if in
the public sphere there are people that
want to believe, and it's a very high
number – higher in Alberta, than perhaps
Ontario, higher still in certain parts of
the United States, like Texas – who
believe that fossil fuels do not
contribute to global warming. But that is
not a credible, academic, scholarly,
scientific position. And to present as if
there's two sides to a debate, when it's
substantially, there is not, an academic,
credible – that becomes problematic. I'm
approaching this from the point of view of
the institution. We are legitimizing
positions that don't have credible
evidence. Just like Charles Murray with
his race claims of white superiority.
Never mind that there is also the issue of
the fact that a certain grouping of
students will be subject to having their
rights subject to what the majority thinks
without... What I'm doing is operating
from a different position here, in saying
that I as a scholar, as someone with
tutorial leaders, I would find it
problematic if my tutorial leaders were
representing positions that didn't have
any substantial academic credibility to
that evidence.

Shepherd: But he's still a public figure.
Yes, he has an academic credential, but
this was on a TV show. He's still a public
figure.

Pimlott: He's a public figure, and there's
a lot of people there like Richard
Spencer, leader of - I don't like calling
them alt-right, it gives them too much
legitimacy -

He glanced at Rambukkana, who nodded approvingly.

Pimlott: But Richard Spencer, right? I
mean... The Nazis actually used - this is
a historical - issues around the free
speech ideas in the 1920s in Weimar,
Germany as an issue around which, which is
what they're using now. We know though
that someone like Richard Spencer is using
theories and ideas which don't have any
academic credibility. He's a public
figure. But in terms of, if we introduce
someone, we give them greater credibility
in a certain condition. Yes, I agree that
there are public figures out there that
bring hatred, that target groups, and if
you look at statistically, the degree of
suicide attempts that trans people, young
people - it's the highest of any group in
society. You go through indigenous people,
right? And so on. There are things that
don't have academic credibility, and I
personally think I have some problems - I
have no problems with the fact that these
things are out there and that people are
going to engage them, but we have to also
think of the atmosphere we also create for
the learning process, right?

Rambukkana: To go back to your question before, "Is it just for those people that are upset about this, or feel threatened by this?" there's something called "the tyranny of the majority." It's that if you want to create an environment that has the ability for everybody to learn, that's not going to block people out just because they are the minority in a particular group, or they might not feel comfortable voicing that they have problems with that material in that space because you're an authority figure in that space. You're also representative of the class, and the department, and the school in that space. Do you understand how it could become an issue? I understand why you made the choice. You wanted to present this as an issue, to talk about, and to bring it out there, et cetera. It's more about trying to understand what the impact of that choice was, and why that might have not been the best choice for this context.

Shepherd: I can see why people would think that. I wouldn't do it again, maybe not this exact case.

Rambukkana: But you would do something similar again? Just, that's your principle, that it would have to be a completely balanced view?

Alas, I was showing signs of being worn down, so they kept pushing.

Shepherd: No. I don't believe a false notion of balance, but I'll say it again, the university is about exposing people to ideas, and I don't get why you have to

47

think a certain way because from what I'm getting in this room, is that if you don't think a certain way, then it's not credible. And not about the academic credibility stuff, but from a public figure point of view. And like I said, I disagree with what he says but I am still open to listening to people. And these students were not open. They're not open to learning new things. Hearing other perspectives.

Rambukkana: So your position is that the students were wrong.

Shepherd: I'm not saying they were wrong, I'm saying they were not open to a new perspective and I find that unfortunate.

Rambukkana: Okay.

Shepherd: Part of university is personal development, and that means becoming a stronger person, and challenging your beliefs and stuff.

Rambukkana: Do you understand how what happened was contrary to, sorry Adria, what was the policy?

Joel: The Gendered and Sexual Violence Policy.

Rambukkana: The Gendered and Sexual Violence Policy. Do you understand how -

Shepherd: Sorry, what did I violate in that policy?

Joel: Gender-based violence, transphobia, in that policy. Causing harm to trans students by bringing their identity as invalid, or their pronouns as invalid, or potentially invalid.

Shepherd: So I caused harm and violence?

Joel: Which is, under the Ontario Human Right Code, a protected thing and also something Laurier holds as a value.

Shepherd: Okay. So by proxy of me showing a YouTube video, I'm transphobic and I caused harm and violence? So be it, I can't do anything to control that.

If they wanted to tell me I had caused harm and violence, then they could tell me that. But their words were so outlandish that they were meaningless to me. There was something sick about being accused of violating a sexual violence policy for discussing pronouns when there were genuine sexual deviants and creeps lurking around on the earth.

Rambukkana: Okay so that's not something that you have an issue with? The fact that that happened? Are you sorry that it happened?

Shepherd: I know in my heart, and I know that I expressed to the class, that I'm not transphobic, and if any of them – again, I don't know what they said – but I don't think I gave away any kind of political position of mine. I remained very neutral.

Rambukkana: That's kind of the problem, is that if you're framing something that's like this – just to give you an example, in lecture I also showed something that was from a member of the alt-right. Were you there for the Guns Unlimited video, talking about the 3D printing, et cetera?

Shepherd: Yep.

Rambukkana: So this is someone who also has a site like the ones that funds Jordan Peterson like Patreon, the alt-right white supremacist website that basically gets funding for these projects if they get kicked off of things like Indiegogo, et cetera. But I framed it by saying those kinds of things, by actually bringing out the critical perspective. To just present information like this neutrally, it can help cultivate an environment where these kinds of opinion, alt-right opinions, white supremacist opinions, anti-trans opinions, anti-gay opinions, anti-women misogynist opinions. Where those can feel like it's a space where those kinds of opinions can be nurtured and created. That's the frame on why some kinds of content we would use in class, or we wouldn't use. Or we would only use those for upper year classes, or grad students. For example, in one of your classes, it might be appropriate to watch a white supremacist recruitment video, something that Richard Spencer has done, because they're students with more critical faculties, that have been exposed to more things that have had more time to process. These are very young students, and something of that nature is not appropriate to that age of student.

Shepherd: 18?

Rambukkana: Yes.

Shepherd: They're adults.

Rambukkana: Yes, but they're very young
adults. They don't have the critical
toolkit to be able to take it apart yet.
This is one of the things that we're
teaching them. This is why it becomes
something that has to be done with a bit
more care.

"Critical toolkit" was a term I had been skeptical of since my
undergraduate years. I heard it quite often in the Communication Studies
department, but it didn't seem to indicate anything other than having the
"correct" viewpoints.

Shepherd: I get what you mean about
framing it. I remember when you talked
about the 3D printing of the guns, and how
you said it was problematic. In
retrospect, yeah I should have used that
word, problematic. That would have been a
good word to bring up.

Who knows why I said that. I suppose I just wanted to get out of that
room instead of go around in circles.

Rambukkana: Well, that's good that you
acknowledge that, especially since you're
saying that this is not something that you
agree with, this is not something that
you're trying to promote. It's just that
you're trying to open up the debate. But
the problem is that that particular debate
is about whether trans people are people
or not. Does that make sense?

Shepherd: It's a language issue, and you
can extend it to whether you want to

extend it to personhood or not. I did
present that argument. I presented the
argument that by denying people their
pronouns you are denying their dignity. I
stated that argument.

From the corner of my eye, I saw Adria Joel lift her eyebrows, as if she
was surprised that I was indeed familiar with different arguments on the
topic.

Rambukkana: But do you understand that if
you were a trans person in that class, or
if the topic was "If women should have the
vote" Do you think you might find that
problematic? Do you think that that might
not be —

Shepherd: [sighs]

Rambukkana: — something that was just
academically related to your identity and
rights, but fundamentally related to your
identity and rights?

Shepherd: Sorry, what's the question
again?

Rambukkana: If you were a trans person in
that class, do you think that that might
not have just been an academic question or
something that was up for debate, but
rather that that was something that
immediately felt impacted you and made the
learning institution that you're paying to
attend a place where you're feeling that
your identity is being questioned and up
for debate?

Shepherd: Would I feel that way if I was a
trans person? It's hard for me to say

because it ties into who people are as individuals and how strong they are and how willing they are to engage with ideas, I don't know if I can make any generalization about –

Rambukkana: Is your position that these students were not strong enough to be able to withstand this kind of critique?

Shepherd: I mean if someone was attacking women in front of me, which it does happen, I feel strong enough in my position to either not respond, and know in my head "Yeah, that person is wrong I'm fine with being a female" but I don't know how other people might react, I don't live in their head, it's hard for me to know.

Rambukkana: Okay, alright, that makes sense.

Pimlott: What I see is, I have not a problem with the idea of debate at any point. What concerns me, of what I know having been here now 16 years, I don't know, the first years have changed – this is a first year class, right? CS101? But what I have found is that one of the things is a notion of confirmation bias. You've heard that phrase?

Shepherd: Mhm.

Pimlott: Because you did Comm Studies at SFU. But one of the things is that a lot of the students coming in already hold very strong opinions, whether or not these are opinions backed up with evidence. Again, I'm just adopting the position of a scholar here. My position is to say, we have these students coming in, they have very strong - in my experience anyway, and I'm teaching them in second year even, they have very strong opinions about x, y, and z, and that's fine, but if they're going to be challenged about those opinions, then it's a much greater deal to do that. The world that Jordan Peterson, Ezra Levant, Rebel Media and that have constructed, I find quite amusing in a way. Because it's almost like the left has won and controls everything, and you're gonna be imprisoned if you don't adopt cultural Marxism, politically correct - the new term, cultural Marxism. I find it practically ludicrous that this is the case, given the political economic realities of Canada, Ontario, Kitchener-Waterloo, this institution, precarious work, et cetera. So I just find it ludicrous that people like Ezra Levant and Jordan Peterson believe that. Maybe they believe in those black helicopters that those conspiracy theorists in the States used to talk about, coming to control world government, okay.

I blinked.

Pimlott: That to me is where a lot of that sort of thinking goes. I do know that there's people that bring in those ideas in the classes I teach. I don't feel that I'm doing my duty to challenge these already-established ideas if what I present in the courses I teach and also in terms of the curriculum that communications studies as a field, as an interdiscipline, of many disciplines - I

don't feel I'm teaching critical
engagement in a world where all the
established dominant institutions in
society reinforce a number of different
types of privileges, perspectives, and
prejudices where the university is one of
the few spaces where we can actually take
people, engage them, challenge them. It's
not challenging the faith-based or family
and other types of structures in society
that they've been inculcated with for
years and years in three hours or one
hour, or 50 minutes. You know in some ways
it isn't gonna be much of a challenge, but
if, in an institution that prides itself
of getting to grips, and having peer-
reviewed academically, social-
scientifically, evidence-based research,
is going to work to confirm the kind of
biases based on stuff that cannot be
substantiated in an academic, credible
way, I find that problematic. And I don't
feel we're doing our job as an
institution, simply because we're
presenting both sides – and again I use
the analogy of climate change. The fossil
fuel industry knew this in the 1970s. It's
like the tobacco companies with lung
cancer, as early as the 1920s, they had a
really strong idea that this was
happening. Further and further research
showed that. I would find it problematic,
given the degree of advertising and power
that the Canadian Association of Petroleum
Producers, that Big Tobacco lobbies, Big
Pharma etcetera, have, through
advertising, through the media you're
studying at SFU, that you're part of the
learning process for students, to just
reinforce the kind of prejudices that

students bring to class That to me, is
something that yes, we need to challenge
them. And I challenge them with ideas that
I don't necessarily believe in in 203, but
because they're substantiated and my
colleagues require me to teach them to
prepare students better for third and
fourth year. I'm happy to teach those
students. I hope it'll make every student,
maybe some, rethink what they think. You
know they can say what they believe,
everyone is entitled to their opinions,
but we have a duty as educators, as
scholars, as academics, even as public
intellectuals, to make sure that we're not
furthering, I would call it charlatanism.
I think Jordan Peterson, particularly, and
I know you're not a fan but I think that
he actually shows a form of charlatanism
when it comes to the academy.

Frankly, the longer this meeting went on, the more of a Jordan Peterson
fan I was becoming.

Pimlott: And he's playing this whole idea
about free speech and public debate which
is not substantiated by the fact that he
has nothing really that is credible in
terms of the research. Including his stuff
on pronouns. And for me, that's where I
find people like Jordan Peterson
problematic, because I don't find anything
credible. I mean there are other people
that teach grammar that could be drawn
upon that could perhaps challenge this
idea of using "they" around the notion of
when you use it. But again, I would say
that that strikes me as a little bit
different bringing in a debate on a
YouTube video about something when we're

56

teaching grammar and talking about
pronouns.

Rambukkana: This kind of brings me back to
the next point, which was kind of thinking
about how to move forward. I can see why
you made that choice, because the topic
was grammar, but your role as TA is not
really to teach about the politics of
grammar, it's to be teaching grammar, to
be teaching punctuation, to be teaching
these things. To be adding clarification
or discussion in relation to the lecture
material, but not to be bringing original
content around side issues, does that make
sense? Has this kind of been your
structure throughout, to bring in more
theoretical aspects around things like
spelling, punctuation, the other topics,
like how to write a thesis statement? Or
was this just this class?

Shepherd: It was just this class. I just
wanted them to see how they interact with
grammar in everyday life. That was how I
framed it. I remember my slide, it said
"Issues in Grammar" and we talked about
English having gendered pronouns, and it
engaged them. People were of all opinion.

Rambukkana: Okay, would you be comfortable
for the rest of the term to stick more to
a more traditional syllabus of teaching
the, maybe not issues around grammar, but
maybe just the particular sentence
structure, whatever the topics are that we
have left?

Shepherd: Mhm. I mean I can't repress my
personality. But I can't see where the

opportunity would arise for me to bring in
another controversial topic.

Rambukkana: Okay. So just thinking
forward, just because of what seems to
have been a little bit of a breakdown in
communication, just about what the
requirements for what the class are - do
you write out your lesson plans or do you
do slides?

Shepherd: Yup, I write them out.

Rambukkana: Okay. Could you send me your
lesson plans before your classes, just so
I can have a quick look over them?

I was now marked as untrustworthy, and would be micromanaged and
surveilled.

Shepherd: I write them on paper, with pen,
but I can take a picture.

Rambukkana: Okay.

Shepherd: But sometimes I don't decide
until, because we get out of the lecture
at 5:50, I have until 8pm to decide what
I'm gonna do based on what you've done. So
I mean I can send it to you literally two
minutes before I start, maybe.

Rambukkana: Okay well, if you can plan,
what we're doing in lecture should be 15
minutes tops of the tutorial. The tutorial
should focus on the skill building. So I'm
assuming that most of that was planned out
more in advance. Like if you have a lesson
on sentence structure, or something.

Shepherd: Today I got them to email me their grammar questions, I'm just going to answer them.

Rambukkana: Okay. Alright. But going forward, if you can maybe try to plan a little further ahead, and then I'm gonna talk about the lecture if that's fine. But send those to me in advance, so I can take a look at them, and if you have any PowerPoint slides, etcetera. I'll ask you not to play any more Jordan Peterson videos, or anything of the like. If you did have something that you wanted to play in class, to let me know ahead of time, so I can take a look. And then I'll also talk everything over with my colleagues and with Peter who's the chair of the undergraduate department. And then we'll talk about how to move forward with this. Does that make any sense?

Shepherd: Sorry that's a little bit vague, could you specify what you mean by moving forward? That's really general.

Rambukkana: Okay. Well, we're going to have to talk about what we said, and then hopefully, everything can continue, and we can continue to have the working relationship that we do but it's something I have to talk over with my colleagues because frankly, some of the things that we talked about are a little bit problematic and we need to process them.

There it was, the accusation that my refusal to fully conform to their ideology was "problematic," and the implied threat of being disciplined or removed from my position.

Shepherd: Do you know when you'll have an answer by?

Rambukkana: I do not.

Shepherd: Okay, but basically you're telling me that the alternative to me continuing my TAship is that it would somehow be terminated? And I'm not sure what the grounds for that would be.

Rambukkana: That's not something that is in my control. I am not your employer, I'm your supervisor. So I have to actually transmit my information, I have to talk about it with Herbert, I have to talk about it with Peter, who is the chair [of the Communication Studies department]. If I knew what the entire process is then I would let you know.

Shepherd: What is the process? What committee is this going to? I kind of need to know where information about me is circulating, and I don't know.

Rambukkana: I don't know either. Herbert?

They were flying by the seat of their pants.

Pimlott: I would only assume that it would be with Peter.

Shepherd: Because you said you have to talk it over with your colleagues so I don't know -

Rambukkana: My colleagues Herbert, Adria, and Peter.

Pimlott: And Peter's the chair of the department. I don't have any say over your TAship in any sense, but what we have to discuss is what we discussed here, and discuss that with Peter.

A journalist who had previously worked in academia later highlighted that exact point to me: Pimlott doesn't have any say over my teaching assistantship. So why was he there?

Joel: Right now I would say that this is an informal process, if it got brought to a formal process, which would be somebody made a formal complaint and wants to go forward with that, then that would look a little bit different. That would be based on either the Gendered Violence Policy or the Harassment and Discrimination Policy and would go through those policies and procedures, which are online and available to you if you want to know what that would look like. Hopefully, it can be resolved informally.

Rambukkana: That's my hope too.

Pimlott: So I guess that's what Nathan was getting at by "moving forward." By his phrase "moving forward" that this is an informal process. This is the first time I've been involved in this process in 16 years, and so I don't even necessarily know what the process is. But part of the reason I wanted to hear your story is because a complaint or complaints were made, and we have to hear, because, you know there's two sides —

Shepherd: There's two sides.

Pimlott: - and so we need to know what
happened from your perspective.

Shepherd: Sure.

Rambukkana: So if you can send me your
lesson plans, and I might need to after
talking it over with Peter, sit in on some
of your tutorials just to assess the space
and see how things are, moving forward. Do
you have any other questions?

That was the real punishment, wasn't it? Being monitored, and being put
into a precarious position where you could be tossed out at any time.

Shepherd: No.

Rambukkana: Alright, thanks for coming in,
Lindsay.

I stood up and looked at the three of them. I had the strongest urge to
blurt out, "Just so you know, I recorded this whole meeting." Fortunately,
I was able to exert some self-control and quietly shut the door behind me.

Upon my exit, I went straight into the washroom down the hall and ran
my hands under hot water for a long time, until they were red. I am not
sure how long I was there. But Rambukkana's weekly class lecture was
about to start, so I shut off the taps and made my way across the campus
to the lecture hall.

By the time I entered the doorway to the class, I had already decided I
would be contacting the media. I no longer cared about my personal
reputation at Wilfrid Laurier University, or whether or not I even
continued at this university. What had transpired in that meeting was, in
my mind, a matter of public interest. Universities are prestigious
institutions of deep societal importance, and each one receives millions of
dollars every year in taxpayer funds. Universities are shaping the minds of
our citizens: alumni go on to occupy positions in government,

policymaking, media, arts and culture, and everything in between. It wasn't right to stifle discussion in an environment dedicated to open inquiry and the pursuit of truth, and it wasn't right to tell a TA that taking a neutral position on a current debate in society was wrong. According to my university superiors, I had broken the provincial human rights code and the sexual assault code simply because I played a clip from public television in class and facilitated an open, nonjudgmental discussion about it. People needed to know this was happening. I wasn't a fool who was going to let the multiple levels of university bureaucracy squash this issue and then be micromanaged until I graduated. If I even made it to graduation, that is.

*

On the first day of TA orientation, back in September, Rambukkana had asked us to refrain from using laptops in his lectures, as he wanted the TAs to set a good example for the students by staying focused on the lecture and promoting the use of handwritten notes, which are better for student learning. If the TAs were scrolling through Facebook during lecture and appeared to not care about the class content, students would figure they didn't have to care about the course content either.

I had always preferred to take my notes by hand anyways, and had done so for years. But it turned out I was the only TA of the eight of us who obeyed Rambukkana's direction. The other TAs had their laptops open throughout the entire lecture from day one. The one TA I sat beside (well, she would very soon begin sitting on the opposite side of the room) would check her email, browse hotels and flights, and surf the web. The other six TAs didn't sit close to me, but whenever I glanced in their direction, they were showing one another their screens – pointing, smiling, and whispering with one another as Rambukkana was speaking at the front of the room.

But on the day after the meeting, I pulled out my laptop in class for the first time ever in Rambukkana's course. I had to act now. I vigorously researched reporters and outlets that might be interested in hearing about what had just transpired: I ended up emailing reporters at the National Post, Waterloo Region Record, and Vancouver Sun. I contacted Christie Blatchford from the National Post, as I saw that one of her speeches at the University of Waterloo had been shouted down in 2010. I hadn't heard of her before, but I figured my case might interest her based on that experience. I copied media baron Conrad Black in the email. I then reached out to the Toronto Sun, the CBC, and the Globe and Mail.

I knew that by going public, I would be relinquishing a certain aspect of control over my own narrative. There was a significant chance that the public would not receive my story well, and I would forever be known as a widely-denounced transphobic bigot if you searched my name online. But, there was also a significant chance that people would understand why I recorded this meeting and felt it was necessary to go public, and I was willing to risk it.

Christie Blatchford emailed me back 40 minutes later, and told me she would call me in the morning.

CHAPTER 5

Christie and I exchanged some initial emails and had a couple of brief phone calls so she could confirm the details of the incident, and ensure she got the facts straight. After I sent her the secretly-recorded audio, she wrote back to me, "I just listened. Jesus H. Christ, what a pompous pair of gits," and "You do realize these people are INSANE?" I was unsure, at that point, whether it was legal for me to have recorded the meeting. I was completely willing to be named in Christie's piece, but I asked her not to mention the recording I sent her. She respected my wishes, and said she would use quotes from the recording without mentioning I had a tape of the conversation. I contacted Jordan Peterson through the email address on his website, explained what happened, and gave him a head's up that I was going to the press, so he shouldn't be shocked if he saw his name in the papers soon.

From the first time I spoke to Christie over the phone, I felt like I was talking to someone with genius levels of perceptiveness – someone who intuitively understood me and immediately understood the issues at hand.

Christie released her article on November 10, 2017, in the National Post. "Thought police strike again as Wilfrid Laurier grad student is chastised for showing Jordan Peterson video," the article was titled. The subheading read "Her supervising professor told her that by showing the video to her 'Canadian Communication in Context' class, 'it basically was like … neutrally playing a speech by Hitler …'"

I read over her article. In the meeting, I had barely even noticed Rambukkana's comment comparing Peterson to Hitler. When you're in a high-stress situation like a disciplinary meeting, some of the most revealing comments can go unnoticed.

By the time I clicked on Christie's article, readers were already pouring into the comment section. Throughout that whole day and the next, I was continually refreshing the comment section, not wanting to miss a single comment. "Long live Jordan Peterson," "RIP Free speech on campus," and "What a world we live in when the 22-year old TA has more sense and courage than those corrupt professors," the comments read. It seemed to me that the verdict was in: I was in the right. There were some comments on the skeptical side: "Sounds like a god-awful situation, but this is just the TA's side of things, we don't know what was really said in that room." Those comments were totally fair: at that point, I had no intention of ever making it known that I had an audio recording of the meeting. At least Christie Blatchford knew that I hadn't twisted any component of the story. My fears about being widely denounced online washed away: the praise was by far outweighing any negative comments.

I sent the Christie Blatchford piece to a couple of my close friends and family members, who all congratulated me for getting the story in the media. Christie also forwarded me some emails from readers who wanted to send me a message of support. I made sure to get my own hard copy of the newspaper for memory's sake – I took the bus over to Conestoga Mall and bought the last National Post from the stands at the convenience store. Sure enough, Christie's column was on page A5. I proudly took the newspaper home and stashed it in a bag of mementos that I kept in my closet, where I put special cards, photos, ticket stubs, and other reminders of meaningful moments.

The next day, Laurier acknowledged the article: they sent out a news release on November 11, 2017 saying simply:[6]

> *The National Post recently published a column that referred to Wilfrid Laurier University. The university is committed to fostering a learning environment that is open and challenging but also welcoming and supportive of all students. The university is engaging a neutral third party to gather facts regarding the situation referenced in the column. Because of the privacy issues involved, we will follow established internal processes. It is important to understand that the issues involved in this matter are complex and affect all universities.*

I didn't think much of the statement, as no one had contacted me about any third-party investigation.

My work was now done. All I had wanted was one single article that exposed the professors, the Communication Studies department, the diversity office, and the preposterousness of the meeting. Christie told me to let her know if I faced any fallout, and thanked me for reaching out. I was feeling rather proud: I had done my part to notify the wider Canadian public about the suppression of free thought in academia. I could die tomorrow knowing that I had made a societal contribution in my life.

However, a second story was in the works: a couple days later, I met with the Waterloo Region Record's Luisa D'Amato at Veritas Café. She was an old-school journalist who knew the ins and outs of the industry: she was the first to confirm to me that my act of covertly recording the meeting was in fact legal. In Canadian privacy law, only one person in the conversation needs to know the conversation is being recorded, and in the Laurier meeting, that one person was me. When she wrote her article, Luisa included the fact that I had recorded the meeting.

Luisa asked me to return to campus that afternoon so that a photographer from the Record could take my photo. I was wearing a magenta-coloured toque that I had bought from the University of British Columbia Botanical Gardens gift shop that summer, along with a blood orange dress and a pink scarf. On Tuesday, November 14, Luisa's article was released: "WLU censures grad student for lesson that used TVO clip."[7]

The day the article came out, I was walking through a hallway at Laurier, glancing over into classroom windows as I often do, to see what kinds of classes were going on. As I walked by one room, I stopped and did a double take: the picture of me in my pink toque and orange dress was being projected onto the screen, with the logo of the Record at the top. The door was closed, as classes had already started that hour, so I could only see the professor's lips moving as she gestured toward the picture of me. I was desperately curious to hear what was being said, but alas, the class size was only 30 or so – I would certainly have been noticed if I had tried to sneak in and sit at the back.

Christie Blatchford notified me that a Laurier liberal arts professor, David Haskell, was looking for my contact information – he had written an op-ed in the Toronto Star that supported me. He wrote:[8]

> *Quotes from the meeting, which Shepherd recorded, show that she was subjected to a barrage of accusations as her motives and character were called into question. She was ultimately told she was not allowed to expose students to views like those of Peterson because, according to her thesis adviser, discussions that create "an unsafe learning environment" are "not up for debate."*

> *To her credit, during her inquisition Shepherd had the courage to suggest that it was not the duty of the university to make students comfortable but to make them think. Had she been given more chance to speak, she might have also noted that claiming certain ideas can make a classroom "unsafe" is, for the most part, an unscientific ruse used by many to simply rationalize censorship.*

Once I got in touch with him, Haskell told me he was in contact with Global TV and could arrange for them to come to campus to film a segment about the Laurier controversy. Haskell was a strong proponent of free expression and open inquiry, and wanted the story to gain more traction. He stressed that TV news got more eyeballs than print news. I agreed to speak on camera.

The Global segment was airing that same evening on the nightly news. I didn't have access to cable in my basement suite, but wanted to watch it right when it aired, so I went to the campus pub that night and asked the bartenders to change the channel to Global. I could hardly hear any sound coming from the speakers, but there I was on the screen, in my pink ski jacket and purple glasses. Being from the Greater Vancouver area, I was accustomed to only wearing a ski jacket in the cold months, with three layers of shirts underneath. Even then, I was still usually freezing. It took me a long time to realize I needed to invest in a puffy parka.

"Hey look, it's Laurier!" a pubgoer exclaimed, pointing to the B-roll on-screen of the campus quad earlier that day.

I then saw a still picture of my face on-screen, with some direct quotes from the meeting, and an audio waveform moving up and down. I realized Global TV had included an excerpt of my original audio recording. I had sent it to them when they asked to review it, but I couldn't recall ever giving explicit permission for them to publicize any part of it. Oh well, nothing I could do about it now.

But once people heard the recording for themselves, even just the small snippet from Global – that's when everything got really, really crazy.

CHAPTER 6

On Monday, November 20, 2017 I woke up shortly after 5:30am – I had to be at CTV's Kitchener studio at 6:30am to appear on their breakfast show, Your Morning.

The studio was quiet and sleepy – Professor David Haskell and I were the only interviewees there. I had already straightened my hair and applied some foundation and mascara at home. But after seeing how pale and washed-out I looked in the studio lighting, I learned to never make that mistake again. If you are invited to do an on-camera interview, always ask for hair and makeup services.

I was led into the studio, a large empty room with one stool set up in front of a green screen, facing the camera equipment. I sat there nervously before the camera operator gave me the signal that we were live, and I heard the voice of TV host Ben Mulroney in my earpiece. I answered the questions coming into my earpiece and pretended I was having a lively face-to-face conversation with Mulroney as I sat alone in a big, dark room and struggled to keep my eyes fixed on the camera in front of me.

The previous week, when only a couple of articles and op-eds had been written about the Laurier affair, it was easy for me to track all of the new comments and get a sense of how people were reacting to the story. But after the audio excerpt was released by Global, and I subsequently gave permission to Tristin Hopper from the National Post to release the entire 42-minute recording, the media coverage became more of a media frenzy. I was doing multiple radio interviews a week, often in between classes. TAs were not given consistent office space at the university, so we used communal offices. When I had an interview scheduled, I would find an empty office and tape a makeshift sign to the door that said "Interview in Progress, Please Do Not Enter."

It is hard to describe what it's like to go from a person receiving two or three emails requiring your attention a day to receiving fifty messages and requests a day, some of them urgent media inquiries. I had emails asking to set up times to be filmed for documentaries and interviewed on podcasts, emails asking me to write guest op-eds, and emails from Laurier students and alumni asking me to meet up over coffee. I had an invitation from classical liberal commentator Dave Rubin to appear on his LA-based show, The Rubin Report. Many people wrote me messages urging me to leave Laurier and find another graduate school: there were even a couple professors who had reached out to me about switching over to their institutions. It had been my first instinct to leave Laurier: I had even told Christie Blatchford I was "about 70 percent sure I will be leaving Wilfrid Laurier after this semester is over." But I knew that Rambukkana, Pimlott, Joel, the Diversity and Equity Office, and the Laurier bureaucracy would love it if I left: there would be no one on the inside seeing what was going on. I was coming to the realization that it would be better to stay.

I was receiving messages of support, requests for phone calls to give people life advice, emails with resources for me to read and watch. I was surprised at how many thoughtful and kind letters of support I received, and surprised at how much they mattered to me and boosted my morale. I couldn't recall any time I had ever reached out to someone and offered them a message of support, and realized I ought to start doing so.

Students were coming to me with stories of political correctness and safe space culture in their classrooms: one psychology student recounted to me how in one of her courses at Wilfrid Laurier University, the instructor announced that white students should try to keep their hands down and not speak as much in their classes as people of colour, because white people are given more opportunities to use their voice outside of the classroom. The student told me how jarring the statement was to her: shouldn't all voices in the classroom be encouraged to speak? An American student sent me screenshots of emails from one of his professors: his class had an exam scheduled the day after the US

71

Presidential election in 2016, and the professor sent an email saying that if anyone was distressed by the election of Donald Trump, they could be exempted from the exam and take it another day. The professor sent a subsequent email expressing surprise at how many students had jumped at that opportunity.

Some old coworkers and acquaintances from British Columbia told me they saw me in the news, and I got a handful of emails from my own CS101 students telling me they support me and know I did nothing wrong. I figured that for at least a few of them, their parents had likely ordered them to write to me, but it was sweet nonetheless.

I was being copied on emails sent to Rambukkana, Pimlott, Joel, and Wilfrid Laurier President Deborah MacLatchy. One such letter forwarded to me, addressed to Prof. Rambukkana, said:

> *It was with considerable dismay that I read the article in the Record concerning Lindsay Shepherd. I believe that, rather than being censured, she should be commended for the initiative she showed in presenting the clip from a respected TVO programme. Let me say from the outset that I do not agree with much of what Jordan Peterson says. However, for a university to stifle honest discussion of ideas which may be offensive to some is contrary to everything a university stands for. Your statement that WLU is currently "blanketed with white supremacist posters" is simply not true. I am frequently on campus and have not seen a single such poster. Staff members whom I have consulted assure me that your claim is false.*

It was always a source of incredible guilt and anguish for me that I wasn't able to reply to each letter of support with the long, thought-out reply that each person deserved. I felt like an ungrateful person for not answering each message, but I just wasn't able to keep up. I will forever be haunted by those unanswered emails.

*

I was reluctant to write Twitter into this book – it felt silly to include happenings from the realm of social media. But it was inevitable that I'd have to do so, as much of the commentary about the Laurier controversy and antagonism that I received took place on the platform. Prior to the Laurier controversy, I did not have a Twitter account, and didn't realize that the Canadian journalism industry lived on this platform. All of these Toronto-based pundits with their blue verification badges were digging around looking for Twitter outrage to write stories about, or using the site to make a name for themselves. I hadn't heard of any of these people before, but apparently, they were important on Twitter, as reified by their blue badges.

I had deleted my Facebook account years prior, as I didn't want to partake in a culture of self-importance, and I had an inactive Tumblr account from when I was a teenager. But as the Laurier media coverage ramped up, it became clear that I would need a mode of communication that I was in control of, so that I didn't need to rely on the media to publish my quotes. Twitter's mini text-based model seemed like the best option.

On November 16, the Canadian Press was reporting that Laurier had officially launched a third-party investigation, and that "Laurier would not confirm what discussions have taken place with Shepherd, but say they have asked an unidentified 'neutral third-party professional' to 'gather the facts' of the case."[9]

I created my Twitter account shortly after reading that article. In my biography section, I wrote "Grad student @ WLU. Made this Twitter to address the Laurier situation in my own words. Otherwise, I do not really use social media."

For my first tweet, I wrote that in fact no discussions had happened between me and Laurier, as I was only finding out about this neutral fact-finding investigation through the news. No one from the university had told me directly that me and my class were officially under investigation.

They had, however, issued a public statement on November 16 titled "Laurier responds to recent media articles" (see Appendix A).

Next, because I was seeing a barrage of comments about how I was an aggrieved conservative with a right-wing agenda, I tweeted "Re: those claiming I have a right-wing agenda: Unfortunately, you have missed the point. Freedom to circulate ideas and debate current affairs is everyone's issue. I am a leftist. But I do not represent the leftism of Rambukkana/Pimlott, who believe in shutting down opposition."

And I did see myself as a leftist, albeit in retrospect, a default leftist. I wasn't religious. I was pro-choice, environmentally-aware, concerned about public transit, affordable housing, and wealth inequality, and had zero qualms with gay marriage. In my mind, those characteristics disqualified me from being a right-winger or a conservative. But even as a self-declared leftist who voted for left-leaning parties in Canada, I was excited when I saw Donald Trump's presidential win announced on TV in 2016, for reasons I can't really explain – the anti-establishment energy of the Make America Great Again movement appealed to me.

"If Americans had a better education system, this wouldn't have happened," a girl in my fourth-year political communication class opined the day after the election.

But that means you're saying a better education will result in everyone having only one opinion or outlook on something, I thought to myself.

I was also rooting for Marine Le Pen in the 2017 French election: while browsing French-language videos on YouTube to practice my listening and comprehension skills, I came across a mainstream media documentary short that was clearly trying to frame Le Pen as a bigot, but I thought she seemed kind of interesting.

Many interviewers were interested in asking about my political orientation, as self-declared left-wing free speech advocates seemed to be more of a rarity than right-wing ones. I came to dread the question of whether I was a right-winger or a left-winger — I started to feel that neither the right-wing or left-wing label applied to me, and I wasn't sure those labels fully applied to most people. I gradually moved away from defining myself as a leftist.

After the third-party investigation kicked off, I saw a clip of a distinguished-looking man with red glasses circulating on Twitter: it was a Toronto employment lawyer named Howard Levitt. On November 21, Levitt appeared on Global TV[10] and said:

> *Steven Paikin, one of the most moderate pundits in the country — playing a clip from his particular show — and finding that that is over the top for the university students to be allowed to listen to, it just strains incredulity. It's incomprehensible in the extreme. It doesn't breach the human rights code… these people have their political views and they try to parade them on some altar of the law which doesn't apply at all… if it was illegal to show both sides of an argument at a university campus, then we wouldn't call this Canada, we'd call this Maoist China at its most extreme.*

"*It just strains incredulity,*" my mom would quote him. "I love the way he says that."

Levitt and I got in touch, and he offered to provide me with pro bono legal advice. He also asked me if I was interested in suing the university, but I was not. We agreed that I would not participate in Laurier's third-party neutral investigation in case of any bias on the part of the university-hired investigator, Rob Centa. Centa would be interviewing some of my CS101 students, as well as presumably Rambukkana, Pimlott, and Joel, so the investigation would still be proceeding, but I would not be sitting down with him.

The next day, I saw another clip making the rounds on social media: Conservative Leader of the Official Opposition Andrew Scheer had mentioned my case on the floor of Parliament.

"Mr. Speaker, will the Prime Minister join me in condemning the egregious crackdown on free speech at Laurier University?" Scheer said as his party stood up and applauded.

Liberal Minister of Science Kirstie Duncan rose to answer. "Mr. Speaker, our government is committed to creating open spaces for Canadians to debate and express their views. In the free society we may disagree with the person's views but we must defend their right to hold them… unless those views promote hate. Intolerance and hate have no place in Canadian society or in our postsecondary institutions."

We defend free speech unless it's hate, and hate is anything we say it is. It was an argument I would become very familiar with.

The conversation was rolling on Facebook as well: a Communication Studies graduate student wrote a post about the Laurier controversy that read:

> *We don't debate about white people being able to use the N word because there is a historical context that makes it wrong. We shouldn't debate about whether or not we should call people by the correct pronouns because there is context as to why this too is wrong. She [Lindsay Shepherd] did not respect and protect the identities and use of language that are now protected by Canadian Law (C-16). Questioning the validity of someone's identity and how it correlates with language is not something that should be taken lightly… Staff talked to the TA because her students issued formal complaints about how the discussion was facilitated.*

I was baffled by the statement, and frustrated to be attending graduate school alongside someone who would make such a bad-faith interpretation of an incident involving a colleague. Worse, she was more interested in getting on her high horse and signalling her own virtuous opinions than bothering to speak to me personally or double check the basic facts of the case. At the risk of sounding harsh, this was exactly the type of individual that was debasing the academic merit of a Master's degree.

Counter to what this graduate student was disseminating, no student had issued any "formal complaints." Even in the original recording, it was specified that the alleged complaints were at an "informal" stage, and that this was an "informal" process.

I couldn't believe that someone who was in graduate school was advocating for a shutdown of debate, and censorship of certain topics. I had been under the impression graduate school attracted the most open, inquisitive, and curious minds, but instead I was finding rigid ideological conformity and disavowal of those who deviate ever so slightly. Not to mention that this student was falling into the familiar cyclical trap of citing Bill C-16 as the reason why Bill C-16 could not be questioned.

Despite being subjected to the occasional negative online screed, I would have felt very alone on campus if it weren't for social media and the internet. When I opened my laptop, prominent individuals were engaging with the Laurier controversy on Twitter: "Hard to imagine that someone actually thought watching The Agenda on a university campus made them feel 'unsafe.' have we really lost the ability to debate issues on campuses?" tweeted Steve Paikin. "I killed myself around minute 25 of the Lindsay Shepherd audio. I'm now tweeting from the other side…" wrote author Sam Harris, whose work I was a fan of. "To call this scandalous is barely to scratch the surface," tweeted Jordan Peterson.

I was also surprised – and flattered – to see that a handful of Conservative MPs and local politicians started following me on Twitter.

I had created a Twitter account because I wanted the opportunity to correct misinformation, address questions, and engage with the broader community. I wanted to be more accountable and allow people to receive information straight from me. But Rambukkana, Pimlott, and Joel had the opposite idea: they went dark. For all intents and purposes,

Rambukkana, Pimlott, and Joel disappeared. Rambukkana deleted his Twitter account[11] and anonymized his Facebook account, and Herbert Pimlott locked down his Twitter account, only briefly leaving up the Facebook page for his female alter ego Hillary X Plimsoll before deleting that account as well. They were not answering any media requests. Whenever I read an article concerning the Laurier affair, it was no surprise to see a variation of the phrase "Rambukkana, Pimlott, and Joel could not be reached for comment" at the bottom of the page.

Days went by with Rambukkana, Pimlott, and Joel hiding from the media, and days soon turned into weeks. I understood the ethical complexities of what I had done by releasing the recording of a private conversation, and that these three individuals suddenly had to face the consequences for their behaviour behind closed doors. I recognize that they were likely blindsided by the public scrutiny and accountability that was being forced upon them. But I couldn't understand their radio silence. For me, personally, if any remarks I had ever made became public, I would feel obliged to address them – to own them and to explain myself.

*

I stepped into my Approaches to Cultural Analysis class after a week of op-eds, radio interviews, and another TV interview. It had now become impossible to avoid acknowledging the nationwide impact of the story. Everyone looked toward the door when they heard it click open. While I may have previously received some small smiles, greetings, or neutral expressions, this time everyone quickly averted their eyes to look at the floor.

Okay then, I thought to myself as I took my usual seat, and swiveled around to face the front of the class. I peered up from my notebook to see one of my classmates staring at me. Right when I looked up at him, he darted his eyes to the floor.

Our professor, Alicia Sliwinski, started off the class with a precursory announcement, that I will paraphrase to the best of my memory.

"Hi everyone. It's going to be a tough class today," she said with a big sigh. "There are some very difficult issues going on, here at the university, but we are just going to have to get through this. I have a class that I have to teach."

I squinted at her. I couldn't even place my finger on why her words were so odd. Perhaps it was because she was implying that my name, and the issues my name now represented at Wilfrid Laurier University, were downright unmentionable. When I saw professor Sliwinski in the hallway later that day, I politely asked her why she had made that announcement before class, and what she had meant by it. Had someone in the class indicated that they were uncomfortable with my presence? "Well," she said to me, "How would you feel if you were on the other side of things right now?"

Later that day, I received an email from a professor from one of my other classes, sent to the whole MA CAST cohort. Even though there were still a couple more weeks to go this semester, our professor, Penelope Ironstone, suddenly announced that we would no longer be required to submit our weekly reading responses, effective immediately, for the rest of the semester. The reading responses were previously public, so everyone in the class could read one another's submissions. I logged onto the class website: the discussion board was now closed, and all the previous submissions had disappeared. I reckon they thought I was a right-wing spy who was going to copy all of their reading response submissions and send them to the Koch brothers.

I saw I had a new message from a classmate: she wrote that she was forbidding me from speaking about her to the media. I am not sure why she thought I found her interesting enough to ever mention in the media – she was a rather unremarkable person. In another instance, I was at a general meeting with the graduate student association, as I had been appointed the Faculty of Liberal Arts Representative in September. A PhD student on the board of directors, who had been sneering at me ever since I walked in the room, announced loudly at the start of the meeting that she did not consent to be recorded. Everyone around the table glanced at me. I had recorded the meeting with Pimlott, Rambukkana and Joel to expose institutional corruption, in a whistleblower-type role. I wasn't going around recording mundane interactions and downloading reading responses to send to some right-wing cabal.

At least one classmate wanted to meet with me, however, and seemingly in good faith.

This classmate asked me to have lunch with her at Wilf's, the campus pub, and talk about what was going on. Because I thought it was a gracious action on her part, I accepted, though not without skepticism.

We engaged in a bit of small talk before turning to the Laurier controversy. My skepticism was somewhat on point: over the course of the lunch, she said I ought to formally apologize to the trans community. I answered, with a slow shake of the head, "I don't have anything to apologize for."

She then mentioned how she noticed my social media following was growing very quickly. Because at the time I only followed two people on Twitter, she told me it would be great if I could follow her, because it would be easy for people to see who I follow and then they could check out her profile. This classmate was always trying to plug her sex therapy consultation business. My memories of her in class are of her announcing she was doing Kegel exercises and none of us even knew it, and bouncing up and down while making exaggerated moaning noises for an uncomfortable length of time while talking about the acting in internet pornography, which is a topic absolutely no one had been discussing.

She insisted on paying for our meal, and we parted on good terms.

I did not follow her on Twitter, as I was not interested in seeing information about dildos, anal sex, and pornography on my timeline. A few months later, she tweeted that she was going to release the full truth about Lindsay Shepherd. I replied, telling her to please go ahead. She immediately blocked me, and decided she would not, after all, release the full truth about me (whatever the supposed "truth" is, I will never know).

*

I nodded to my CS101 class as I entered my classroom: it was time to teach my first tutorial since the media frenzy had erupted. The chair of the Communication Studies department, Peter Urquhart, was already in the room. He stood at the front of the class and made an announcement similar to Professor Sliwinski's: "I want to acknowledge this situation, and tell you that the issue is complex," he said. He said he wanted to "acknowledge that the situation is challenging for all those involved," and then outlined the "supports" for students who found the "situation" to be "challenging."

After his spiel, he opened up the floor for students to ask him questions. The students stared up at him blankly.

"Anyone?" he asked.

The students looked at him in a semi-amused, semi-bored manner.

"Nothing, huh? Alright," he said, slinking to the back of the room, and pulling out his notebook to take notes on my teaching.

That week, the subject was punctuation.

First, I taught the students an important skill: how to successfully integrate semicolons into their writing. I got the students to take out a piece of lined paper and come up with a sentence that used a semicolon, and told them to hand it to me before they left class for the day.

I also talked about apostrophes, and how they should never be used to make a word plural.

"Which sentence is correct?" I asked my class.

> *Research has shown that student's who attend class regularly attain higher grades.*

> *Research has shown that students who attend class regularly attain higher grades.*

Yes, even in university writing, these were items of concern. I then brought up how to properly integrate quotation marks into a phrase, and for fun showed a couple of memes where quotation marks were improperly and thus humorously placed, such as on a sign that read "Employees Must 'Wash' Hands" photographed in a restaurant.

Because I knew in advance that Urquhart would be sitting in on one of my classes, I decided to have a bit of light-hearted fun. My next slide read "Controversy????"

"Okay everyone," I sighed, "We're going to talk about a major controversy now."

I paused to create some tension. I received a few bewildered looks.

I switched to my next slide: "The Oxford Comma!"

At the end of class, as the students shuffled their papers and handed in their deliverables at the front of the room, Peter Urquhart walked by me and said, a bit begrudgingly, "Good job today." And I had done a good job. But his compliment was uttered in such an ambiguous way that I thought perhaps, he had entered my classroom today with the expectation that I was an incompetent teacher – an insensitive and low-emotional intelligence person who couldn't read the room, or someone who used class time to spout off on whatever I wanted instead of sticking to relevant topics. I think I detected ambiguity in his voice because he was realizing that the apparent characterizations of me that were circulating the department, and the entire university, were simply not the case, and he didn't really know what to think anymore.

CHAPTER 7

When I arrived on campus the following week, posters were plastered on the doors, walls, and bulletin boards of all the main buildings.

"WHAT HAPPENED TO LAURIER'S GENDERED & SEXUAL VIOLENCE POLICY? TRANS STUDENTS DESERVE AN APOLOGY" they read.

Some said only, "TRANS STUDENTS DESERVE AN APOLOGY."

The on-campus LGBTQ hub, the Rainbow Centre, had a new sign in their office window as well, facing out to the main quad: "TRANS STUDENTS DESERVE AN APOLOGY," hand-painted in dark writing – but the word "DESERVE" in blood red.

As it turns out, both President MacLatchy and Nathan Rambukkana had issued apologies to me that day, and the campus activists were upset that they hadn't received a set of apologies as well.

I regarded apology letters, in general, as bureaucracy-crafted statements that were just meant to prevent any further embarrassment. Therefore, I never paid much attention to apology letters. But I had to quickly read Rambukkana and MacLatchy's letters and develop an opinion on them, because the media were blowing up my phone asking for comment. "Just give me 10 minutes," I'd plead with the reporters that called me. Once one or two reporters knew your phone number, it seemed that it circulated to all of them. "I haven't even read the thing yet." I really needed at least an hour to read, think, and reflect on the apology statements; but I let the journalists pressure me into abiding by their timelines.

President Deborah MacLatchy's letter read:

Nov. 21, 2017

I'm writing to make an apology on behalf of the university.

Through the media, we have now had the opportunity to hear the full recording of the meeting that took place at Wilfrid Laurier University.

After listening to this recording, an apology is in order. The conversation I heard does not reflect the values and practices to which Laurier aspires. I am sorry it occurred in the way that it did and I regret the impact it had on Lindsay Shepherd. I will convey my apology to her directly. Professor Rambukkana has also chosen to apologize to Lindsay Shepherd about the way the meeting was conducted.

I remain troubled by the way faculty, staff and students involved in this situation have been targeted with extreme vitriol. Supports are in place at the university to support them through this situation.

[...]

Let me be clear by stating that Laurier is committed to the abiding principles of freedom of speech and freedom of expression. Giving life to these principles while respecting fundamentally important human rights and our institutional values of diversity and inclusion, is not a simple matter. The intense media interest points to a highly polarizing and very complicated set of issues that is affecting universities across the democratic world. The polarizing nature of the current debate does not do justice to the complexity of issues.

Laurier is prepared to engage with these important discussions in a thoughtful and determined way. I have announced a task force to delve into these issues. Further details will be announced in the days ahead. I look forward to the process and I am confident that the outcome will contribute to

*a better understanding of these issues for Laurier and the broader
community.*

Why would a university need to strike a task force on freedom of
expression? Freedom of expression is a founding principle of the
academy: an academic institution did not need to establish a task force to
investigate how much one of its own founding principles mattered. It was
just a way to avoid taking any definitive stance and kick the can down the
road. What mattered to me was not whether Laurier apologized to me,
but whether they would commit to fostering a pro-open inquiry
environment from that point onwards. (And I would learn, in the months
ahead, that they had no intention of fostering such a climate.)

I was equally unmoved by Rambukkana's apology letter, released the
same day. He was, predictably, doing what he could to keep his job. More
interesting to me was the fact that Rambukkana had released a public
apology, but Pimlott and Joel hadn't. They had all been present in the
meeting and complicit in accusing me of breaking the law by having an
open academic discussion, so why did Pimlott and Joel get to offload
their wrongdoing onto Rambukkana?

Professor Rambukkana wrote (see full letter in Appendix B):

> *First, I wanted to say that when I was made aware of the concerns, I was
> told that the proper procedure would be to have an informal meeting to
> discuss it. In the process of arranging this, others indicated they should attend
> as well. This is one of the facets of working at a university, that meetings can
> often become de-facto committees due to relevant stakeholders being pulled in.*

It was an apology written in bureaucratese, approved by multiple levels of
university PR and communications officials. The use of the term
"relevant stakeholders" was pretty well proof of that. The letter danced
around the facts, never addressing the route the "complaint" had taken.
Well, actually, it now appeared the "complaints" had been definitively

downgraded to "concerns." So who had the "concerns"? Who did the "concerns" travel through? Who got involved? Why?

> *However, in not also prioritizing my mentorship role as the course director and your supervisor, I didn't do enough to try to support you in this meeting, which I deeply regret. I should have seen how meeting with a panel of three people would be an intimidating situation and not invite a productive discussion.*

For many people following the controversy, what first stuck out to them was the three-against-one dynamic – Rambukkana, Pimlott, and Joel versus me. Some questioned why I was not offered a "support person" or representative, and wondered why the TA union representative was not there – but graduate students at Laurier were not unionized. Some even went so far as to say that two male professors bullied and ganged up on a lone, vulnerable female graduate student. But it had not occurred to me before, during, or after the meeting that I should ask for representation.

Rambukkana's apology went on to emphasize the importance of "contextualizing difficult material." Was this not just another way of saying we must instill the "correct" viewpoints in the students, and all other perspectives must be stamped as "suspicious" or "unacceptable"? Rambukkana, in his apology, stated Peterson's views were "controversial" and must "be handled carefully, especially so as to not infringe on the rights of any of our students or make them feel unwelcome in the learning environment." He was still holding onto the idea that Peterson's views were uniquely dangerous and controversial, and capable of making students feel "unsafe."

Following the apologies, Toronto-based NOW Magazine published an article with the headline "Alt-right's new hero on campus bullies Laurier into an apology."[12]

"It's a sad day when the president and a professor of a university are forced to throw themselves at the feet of those who have made other students feel unsafe in a classroom," the article said.

"Shepherd has recently created a Twitter account to describe 'the Laurier situation in [her] own words.' Despite the fact she says she doesn't use social media, she has found time to target individuals on dozens of occasions who were in disagreement with her, using her recently acquired fan base of 18,000-plus followers to drive hateful comments at her detractors (just as pro-Peterson types like to do)," it continued.

"For too long, folks have marginalized and harmed trans students in the name of free speech and debate. Shepherd's actions continue this trend."

I discovered that the journalist-writer-activist class was very preoccupied with the size of someone's Twitter following, and if you had a relatively sizable following, they would claim that you are weaponizing your account to target and harass those with smaller accounts than yours. The smaller accounts were of course permitted to direct as much vitriol as they wanted to anyone of their choosing.

A writer in Canadian Dimension (a relatively obscure publication, mind you) pumped out an article very similar to the one in NOW Magazine:[13]

> *Canada's punditry just created the world's newest alt-right folk hero. And it only took them 10 days.*
>
> *That has to be a record for them, really quite the feat.*
>
> *Here's a quick primer on the ever-growing dumpster fire: Lindsay Shepherd, a 22-year-old teaching assistant at Wilfrid Laurier University in Waterloo, showed a video of notorious transphobe and alt-right sympathizer Jordan Peterson to a class of first-year communications students. At least one student complained that it was inappropriate to display such content without sufficient context.*

Shepherd was then pulled into a meeting with three academic staff, which concluded with her being instructed to show all future media and seminar notes to her supervisor prior to teaching.

Then, she leaked secretly recorded audio of the meeting to the media.

The punditry immediately exploded. Almost every major commentator, including many self-described progressives, wrote a steaming hot take. The thesis was universal: Shepherd was a free speech hero, faculty and admin were censoring her and gender pronouns are very much up for debate in the classroom. Her freshly created Twitter account racked up thousands of followers in mere days: she now has more than 15,000 followers.

No mainstream pundit stopped to think about what they might be creating until it was too late. And in showing such unabashed support, they outed themselves — once again — as willing accessories to transphobia, white supremacy, and ongoing colonial violence.

In one letter to the Star,[14] (a paper that had just run an editorial in favour of free speech), George Brown College faculty member Griffin Epstein wrote:

> *I am an academic working as an independent researcher and full-time faculty at George Brown College. I have an MA and PhD from the University of Toronto. I am writing to express my disappointment and concern with your coverage of recent incidents involving Wilfrid Laurier University Prof. Nathan Rambukkana and teaching assistant Lindsay Shepherd.*
>
> *Under the guise of protecting free speech, you published content that bullied Prof. Rambukkana, as well as the university at large, into apologizing for an act of intervention that was neither unfair nor unwarranted. Instead of taking a stand against hate speech, you have given dangerous credence to the views of (University of Toronto Prof.) Jordan Peterson and his supporters, flying in the face of the Canadian Charter of Rights and Freedoms...*

As recognized by federal law and nearly all progressive social institutions, gender pronouns are a basic site of self-representation. Peterson's brazen disdain for these protections is a violation of the human rights of students with non-normative identities.

When Shepherd was reported for showing the video, Prof. Rambukkana acted as he should have: by challenging her pedagogy and working to make his classroom safer...

I urge you to reconsider your position on this matter and demonstrate public support for Prof. Rambukkana and his brave stance against hate speech in the classroom.

I almost would have thought it was an exercise in satire, but I googled Griffin Epstein and saw that they had earned their PhD in Social Justice Education at the notoriously ideological Ontario Institute for Studies in Education (OISE) and that they write extensively about identity issues.

About two weeks after the Laurier story had broken, I checked my email and saw a note from Prof. Haskell, who notified me that a group of University of Waterloo and Laurier students were organizing a free speech rally that Friday in my support, at the small Veteran's Green park across the street from the Laurier campus. I met with the students, who were all part of their campus Conservative clubs. They had printed purple-and-gold signs and buttons that said "I Stand With Lindsay" and "I Support Free Speech," and they had gotten a couple local conservative politicians to agree to attend and speak at the rally.

The students requested that I deliver a short speech as well, and I obliged. I had also been corresponding with a Maclean's reporter who wanted to do a profile of me for the magazine and asked to tag along with me for a day, if I still hung out on campus.

"I do hang around campus, but don't really interact with anyone or go anywhere, to be honest. I just stay in an office. But if you want to come down to campus that certainly works. The only interesting upcoming thing is a free speech rally I will be speaking at on Friday," I wrote to him.

"That sounds like something definitely worth going to," the reporter, Aaron Hutchins, replied.

CHAPTER 8

Free speech was, frankly, not an issue I had ever given much deep consideration before the Laurier controversy. I thought constantly about open discussion; but more in a humanistic than political or rights-based sense. I had always wondered why so few people were capable of carrying an interesting and thoughtful conversation, and why so many people seemed afraid to talk about what really mattered and were instead drawn to the trivial; only interested in what they could consume. It seemed to me that so many people were afraid of saying the wrong thing, making honest conversations limited in their depth. It was difficult to obtain a conversation partner who was nonjudgmental and imaginative, and who knew how to balance humour and gravitas. Some people had a spark and a wit about them: you knew they were registering and thinking about what you were saying. Other people had an emptiness about them – they lacked reaction and response time, in spite of being mentally competent, and it seemed you weren't understanding one another even though you were both speaking the same language.

As a student at Simon Fraser University, I had once passed by a booth on Clubs Day that had some sort of banner or poster about saving free speech. *Free speech*, I thought to myself. *That's a strange issue to champion.* Surely anyone championing free speech is a misfit with some odd, marginal opinions, and they're just trying to protect their ability to express them.

Having spent the majority of my undergraduate years working in low-paying or low-status jobs, the issues that kept me up at night had more to do with labour, status, and class. I would wonder why so many customers I encountered thought less of people who worked behind the counter. In my spare time, I would empathetically read blogs where workers recounted their stories of being mistreated in the service industry.

Of course, working in the service industry was not all bad. One year, at the gelato shop I worked at, a single mouse had chosen to make its home underneath one of our mixing machines for several weeks. A 50-something man donning a suit and briefcase came into the shop, and as I was handing him his order, the mouse scurried across the floor in plain sight. I froze, thinking the man was going to yell at me, demand a refund, and accuse the store of being unhygienic. Instead, he licked the gelato off his cone, and said thoughtfully, "That little guy's just trying to survive, like the rest of us."

I was of the opinion that every job in society was part of a larger ecosystem, and therefore no one doing honest work should ever be looked down upon. It's an opinion that made me sympathetic to communism, as I thought that was the only system that would honour the importance of all lines of work. (Of course, I would learn that leftists denigrated people based on class as well: I was receiving comments online from Marxists and leftists about how I was too stupid to be a graduate student, and I would eventually end up working at Starbucks).

Sometimes, to explore my future job prospects, I would browse online job boards and wonder why ads for entry-level jobs required at least three years of relevant experience. Meanwhile, wages were low and the cost of living was high. I thought about what it would take to get ahead in this country – but ugh, I hated the phrase "get ahead." I wasn't trying to get ahead of anyone, I wanted everyone to be doing well for themselves.

All of my professors spoke ominously about the gig economy my classmates and I would be facing: a life of precarious work, jumping from short-term contract to short-term contract, with no benefits or sense of permanence. Though my professors suggested a bleak future was in store for us, I liked the idea of working numerous temporary and part-time jobs. It was more exciting – it would expose you to more skills, characters, and settings.

After the Laurier controversy broke, people wanted to hear my opinion on things aside from just free speech – and they particularly wanted to know my opinion on transgenderism. They likely assumed I had some sort of investment in the issue, and that was why I chose to screen the video that I did. But alas, I did not have a stake in the issue, at least not at the time I showed the TVO clip. Prior to the Laurier affair, if someone had confronted me and asked me "Are transwomen women?" I probably would have shrugged and answered yes. (Though having now steeped myself in the subject and done my research, I would answer no). I knew of a couple past friends and acquaintances from my childhood who had become trans, but I was indifferent to it. The only reaction I had was "Huh, who would have known?" I would think about what they had been dealing with internally that no one had even been aware of.

*

I had never spoken at a rally before. I jotted down my speaking notes on a piece of scrap paper over a cider at the campus pub, finishing only seconds before I had to run across the street to Veteran's Green, where a crowd of about 150 had formed.

Stepping up onto a large rock to deliver my short speech, I urged the crowd to not forget the need for free inquiry, as it is through open discussion that we form and refine our ideas and become the people we want to be. From my perch, I could see a group of 35 or so lining the sidewalk across the street, gathered for a silent counter-demonstration. They donned bibs reading "Trans Students Deserve Justice." I lamented that a dichotomy of free speech versus trans rights had been set up, and was manifesting spatially as if these values were diametrically opposed – they are not.

Immediately after the rally, a producer from the CBC approached me from within the audience and asked if I would go to Toronto to be on the CBC's flagship live news show, The National, that evening.

I hesitated. "I don't drive, how will I get there?" I asked.

"We'll send an Uber over here in about half an hour to pick you up, and we'll send you back in an Uber as well." Downtown Toronto was about a 1.5 hour drive away. "Does that work?"

I wouldn't even have time to go home to shower, change, or eat. I was wearing a black mock neck sweatshirt under my jacket – I suppose that would look presentable. I had jeans and scuffed-up ankle boots on, but that wouldn't show on camera.

"We have hair and makeup at the studio," the producer assured me.

"Okay, I'll do it," I said.

"Great! I'll call the Uber and text you when it's here."

The reporter and photographer from Maclean's were still tagging along, and we used the last half hour to take photos for the magazine profile, before I had to run out to the Uber.

*

The Uber arrived in Toronto, and I stepped into the impressive downtown Toronto studio of the CBC. The host of The National who would be my interviewer, Ian Hanomansing, greeted me. I had seen him on TV many times.

"I personally requested to invite you here on the show. I have children your age in university and I was so impressed by your story, and how well you've been handling this," he told me. We approached the studio, snapped a photo together, and then we were live.

The thought of walking into a live national news studio, last minute and without any prior preparation, is pretty wild, but it was my modus operandi. I didn't have to prepare anything, because I only had to answer questions honestly and openly, which didn't require a PR team.

Right after I finished the interview, the same Uber was waiting outside the studio to shuttle me back to Waterloo. The driver was concerned when I mentioned I had barely eaten anything all day, so he bought me a bagel and tea from the Tim Hortons drive-thru.

When I got home, I snapped a few photos of myself as a souvenir from my evening at the CBC studio, as I hadn't had my hair and makeup professionally done since I was a teenager in a wedding party. The makeup artist had filled in my eyebrows, coated my eyelashes in mascara, curled my hair, and given me a full face of foundation and a slight lip tint.

The CBC producer had encouraged me to take advantage of my done-up hair and makeup and have a night out on the town, but I had nowhere to go. I wiped all the makeup off: the person staring back at me in the mirror was pale, gaunt, and puffy-eyed, with one eyelid drooping more than the other. I had purple rings around my eyes. The contrast of my made-up self and my makeup-less self was so funny that I took some before and after shots.

For many a night those past weeks, I was falling asleep fully clothed in my outfit from the previous day, with my lights on and laptop open on my bed. I would wake up with dry contact lenses in my eyes. Sometimes I would stay up studying until 4am, other days I would go to sleep earlier but wake up at 4am to get my readings done before leaving for class in the morning. It was a pace of life very different from my first easy two months of grad school, and it's why I looked so tired.

When I went home that Christmas, I showed my mom the pictures of the hair and makeup from the CBC studio, which she cooed at appreciatively. I then turned my phone toward her and showed her the picture of me after I had wiped all the makeup off.

"Who's that?" she asked.

"It's *me!*" I cackled.

"What? Let me see that," she said.

"It's me, the same day, just tired and with all the makeup washed off," I explained.

"The same day!" she said in disbelief, laughing along with me.

One of the ways to tell whether someone is in touch with reality or not is to examine how sensitive, defensive, or delusional they are about their appearance. Meeting someone who was entirely objective about their appearance was rare, but I liked to think I was one of those people. It came in handy when people commented on YouTube videos of my interviews. The first comment I ever read about my appearance was, "I had no idea Lindsay Shepherd was a fucking giraffe," in reference to my long neck. I slapped my knees in laughter. I liked having a long neck, in any case – it was certainly preferable to having a short neck. My friend Cosmin, who later became my boyfriend and is now my husband, bought me a little stuffed giraffe after he returned from a trip he went on, as giraffes had become a little inside joke. Some commenters would note how pale I am, and another commenter noted I had an asymmetrical face, but that at least it looked kind of cute on me. I did indeed have an asymmetrical face, and it was nice that the commenter had a positive spin on it. You can't really be offended about anything related to your appearance if you are realistic about what you look like.

CHAPTER 9

After the free speech rally, I sought out all the media coverage to see how it had been portrayed. First, I clicked on a video of the silent "Trans People Deserve Justice" demonstration across the street, posted by the Laurier Students' Public Interest Research Group (LSPIRG), an on-campus leftist activist collective funded by student fees.[15] I was familiar with PIRGs: at SFU, the SFPIRG was always putting up posters about decolonization, intersectional feminism, and fatphobia.

LSPIRG's video featured Rainbow Centre coordinators Toby Finlay and Milas Hewson, who both introduced themselves to the camera with "they/them" pronouns, stating that the silent action they organized was intended to visually represent the silencing of trans and non-binary voices by the free speech debate.

"We're a group of trans and non-binary students who are here to say that trans students deserve justice and to do a silent action against the silencing of trans peoples' voices within both the institutional conversation as well as within the larger media," Toby explained.

"Trans voices have been silenced in a number of ways, first of all by the ways that this free speech discourse has been used to cover up the transphobia that's at the core of these conversations," added Milas.

"We think it's really important that trans people's voices and the impact that this situation has had on trans people are reintroduced to the conversation, I think that the conversation's been taken up in ways that have erased the transphobia really at the core of the situation from this broader discourse," said Toby, reinforcing the same point.

The Rainbow Centre affiliates were claiming that transphobia was "at the core" or "at the centre" of the Laurier affair. I suppose it was their job to advocate for that position, in order to access more resources through their claimed hardship and grievances. But were they not at all concerned about academic freedom or the strength of our academic institutions? The ability to openly question and discuss ideas? The right to pursue truth even when it is uncomfortable?

It wasn't intellectually honest to characterize the Laurier affair as being about "transphobia": such a presumption only served to shut down legitimate discussion about free thought and free expression.

The camera panned to show all of the silent protesters. One woman, wearing a "Trans People Deserve Justice" bib, waved enthusiastically, but was then heard saying quietly to the protester beside her, "Am I allowed to wave?"

At the end of the video, the narrator turned the camera toward the free speech rally, and stated, before signing off, "This is the free speech rally that is actually silencing trans and non-binary students."

In a Globe and Mail write-up about the free speech rally, Toby was quoted as saying "In light of all the media attention that has been brought to Lindsay Shepherd [and] in light of the understanding of transphobia, the needs of trans students and their voices have been silenced."[16]

It wasn't only Toby and Milas who were using this line of reasoning. "It's our voices that are actively being silenced...Freedom of speech is an interesting thing – it only works for those who already have a voice and a platform," Jay Rideout, LSPIRG communications and outreach director, wrote in a NOW Magazine article titled "Its [sic] trans students and staff who deserve an apology from Wilfred [sic] Laurier University."[17]

Time and time again, the trans activists would be on camera, or quoted in print articles, using the platform they had been provided with to argue that they didn't have a voice, and their voices were being silenced. On Twitter, someone created a meme that depicted Toby and Milas encircled by a dozen microphones with mainstream media logos on them, with the caption "Our voices are being silenced!" Sometimes, a meme was better at portraying irony than words.

"The reality of transphobia at the issue's core has been totally silenced," Toby said to the Record.[18] The article went on: "Finlay and fellow student Milas Hewson, who also does not identify with a traditional gender, both say they are in favour of freedom of speech, but it must be from a position of respect."

Toby also told the media that he had been informed "fascists who had been violent in other demonstrations" were attending the free speech rally.[19] My head spun. What fascists? Where were they? Why were these people always claiming fascists and white supremacists were lurking around on campus everywhere?

Laurier Communication Studies professor Jonathan Finn stated that on the day of the free speech rally, he was "advised by colleagues not to come to campus." An anonymous Laurier student also claimed in a blog that "profs cancel[led] our classes last Friday due to a free speech rally happening on campus & we feared for our own safety, & a lot of faculty members & grad students from the Communication program feel unsafe to come to campus."[20]

"Our campus is not safe right now. People feel exposed and threatened. It is a sad place to be. People have been silenced out of fear of being attacked. It is hypocritical that some of those attacking us are claiming to be proponents of free speech," Greg Bird, a professor in my home department of MA CAST, told the student newspaper.[21]

In spite of the terror these people felt, Joseph Brean from the National Post described how the rally proceeded:[22]

> But in the end, the rally at Laurier in support of teaching assistant Lindsay Shepherd, who controversially showed her class an episode of The Agenda on inclusive pronouns, went off like the mildest of campus pep rallies.

The closest thing to civil unrest was a dog off its leash. Not more than three passing cars honked. There was not even much weed in the air.

*

Following the free speech rally, the story of the Laurier affair entered a new phase – a phase of open letters, petitions, and social media statements, accompanied by ramped-up claims of out-of-control violence and harassment on the Wilfrid Laurier University campus.

The Rainbow Centre affiliates were drumming up the media by claiming they were being subject to vicious harassment on campus. "Rancour of free speech debate led gender-diverse people to feel unsafe, advocates say," one CBC article was titled.[23] In the article, professor Greg Bird finally shed some light onto what kind of supposed harassment was happening on campus. Bird stated, "A lot of people are being attacked through phone calls… work emails and much more on our campus by some pretty violent and extreme people out there."

"Faculty and staff are scared to come to work right now," Bird told the Record. "Some professors are receiving threats, extensive rants on their work phones and work emails, and much more."[24]

I quoted Bird to journalist Luisa D'Amato, and she hooted with laughter. "Extensive rants on their work phones? Welcome to my world. That's just an average Tuesday."

As Bird was decrying to the media that the Laurier campus was a house of horrors, he circulated an online petition on behalf of several faculty members claiming the Wilfrid Laurier University campus was unsafe."[25]

The petition read:

We are Wilfrid Laurier University faculty members who are troubled by the events that have recently taken place on our campus and the impacts on trans, non-binary, and gender diverse students and faculty.

Wilfrid Laurier University students and faculty are now being subjected to threats of violence, harassment, intimidation, and our campuses have become unsafe.

We are concerned that little has been done to ensure that members of our community are being protected. If we cannot dedicate more resources, provide a more comprehensive response, and speak against these acts in clear and unequivocal terms, we will be perceived as tolerating these acts. Our university has a duty to uphold the principles of diversity and equity, to foster a culture of inclusion, and to provide institutional support.

We call on the administration to immediately:

1.   *Issue a statement that these actions will not be tolerated on our campus. That transphobia and all other forms of hate targeting persons on the basis of gender identity and expression are being carefully monitored and actions of harassment are reported to the relevant authorities.*

2.   *Establish measures to ensure the safety and protection of students and faculty who are being subjected to discrimination, harassment, and threats on their lives.*

Bird's petition garnered nearly 500 signatures. The Rainbow Centre was making similar claims on their Facebook page:[26]

Dear Laurier Community,

In the face of recent media attention, we feel it is our responsibility to speak out against the climate of transphobia that is being fostered at Laurier. The university's silence on these issues has allowed for a one-sided perspective to be cultivated in the media that is entirely disconnected from the experiences of trans people. We speak now as a collective of queer and trans students, asking you to engage critically with the media you read and to hold our community with care.

[...]

Under the banner of freedom of speech, the news media have advanced a critique of institutional practices aimed at increasing inclusivity and challenging oppression. The always present but often unnamed 'other' at the center of these critiques, [sic] are the trans and non-binary individuals who these institutional practices would support. We must understand the ways in which these attacks on the "PC culture" of the university are, in actuality, attacks on the needs of trans people that these critics do not support.

The discourse of freedom of speech, [sic] is being used to cover over the underlying reality of transphobia that is so deeply ingrained in our contemporary political context. Ironically, these discourses seem intent on silencing those who speak out against the systemic violence perpetrated against trans people while propagating a far right ideology.

We must, therefore, be critical of the ways in which trans bodies are being appropriated as the battleground on which the war of freedom of speech is waged. Debates about gender neutral pronouns or the validity of trans identities are not only discussions about (dis)allowable speech but, also, affronts on the reality of trans experience. These debates, regardless of how "neutrally" they are presented, constitute a form of epistemic violence that dehumanizes trans people by denying the validity of trans experience.

For trans people, these debates invalidate their gender identity or expression as wrong or pathological, with very material impacts for their well-being. According to a national study, two-thirds of trans youth in Canada have engaged in self-harm and one-third have attempted suicide (Veale et al., 2015). For cisgender (non-trans) people, these debates validate the ideologies of cisnormativity and genderism that inform transphobia, once again with material impacts for trans people. According to the Trans Pulse project, for example, 20% of trans people in Ontario have been physically or sexually assaulted for being trans and 34% have been verbally threatened or harassed (Bauer & Scheim, 2015).

In this context, we must respond to the enactment and maintenance of transphobia and problematize media that upholds transphobic ideologies. We should take students' concerns about their safety and well-being as a result of the intensification of these ideologies on campus very seriously. These concerns are real, with students accessing the Rainbow Centre for support around experiences of harassment in their classrooms, on campus, and in online forms, as a result of this increased media attention. The Rainbow Centre itself is being targeted on this issue, with antagonizing posters being left on our windows and emails criticizing our educational initiatives around Transgender Day of Remembrance.

These experiences of transphobia and their aforementioned implications, are the realities in which our conversations about this issue need to be embedded. We all have a responsibility to create an environment for learning and living in which trans people are safe from epistemic and transphobic violence. We all have a responsibility to speak out about these issues, and we call on our allies who have remained silent to please take a stance. This political moment is intent on derogating trans people in the name of freedom of speech and we cannot allow for this profound violence to be continued.

The letter then encouraged individuals "requiring support" to contact the Rainbow Centre's Sexual Violence Support Advocate.

I started to notice, after the release of this statement, how trans activists would almost always invoke rates of trans suicide whenever they were advocating for their position. It was a sort of veiled threat: "do what we want, or you're complicit in the suicide of trans people." Even a neutral discussion about how new pronoun usage might change the English language constituted "epistemic violence that dehumanizes trans people by denying the validity of trans experience."

But as Jonathan Rauch wrote in his 1993 book "Kindly Inquisitors,"[27]

> *If you are inclined to equate verbal offense with physical violence, think again about the logic of your position. If hurtful opinions are violence, then painful criticism is violence. In other words, on the humanitarian premise, science itself is a form of violence. What do you do about violence? You establish policing authorities—public or private—to stop it and to punish the perpetrators. You set up authorities empowered to weed out hurtful ideas and speech. In other words: an inquisition.*

The Rainbow Centre was claiming students were being subjected to harassment in classrooms and on campus due to the "increased media attention," but their claims were never substantiated. They did not come forward with evidence nor did they provide credible examples of real harassment. The Rainbow Centre also claimed they were being "targeted" because they received "emails criticizing our educational initiatives around Transgender Day of Remembrance." But in what world is receiving negative feedback via email about your centre's programming considered "targeting?" And as for the "antagonizing" posters being left on their windows, the only incident I had heard of was that one single poster reading "It's OK to Show Jordan Peterson Videos" was put up on their window and taken down in a matter of minutes.

I suppose I was mostly surprised at their language of "safety" and "support": I hated more than anything when people were condescending to me, when people infantilized me. I couldn't fathom why individuals my age, pursuing (and paying for) a university education, were asking to be treated like they couldn't handle an adult discussion.

At least someone echoed my feelings: reporter Luisa D'Amato wrote a column that interviewed Lyn McGinnis, a local 60-something LGBTQ individual.[28]

> *Lyn McGinnis of Waterloo, who is bisexual and gender-variant, studied at University of Waterloo in the 1980s and 1990s. That was before there were gay-straight alliances, gender-neutral washrooms, or before anyone had a clue that you could declare yourself "non-binary" when it came to gender.*
> *If there were struggles to become accepted, it just made McGinnis, now 62, stronger.*
>
> *But "I don't recognize the culture now. It's turned into a monster."*
> *McGinnis thinks LGTBQ students are being "infantilized, as if they're weak, helpless, utterly fragile" in the bid to create safe spaces on campus.*
> *As for gender-neutral language not being up for debate, "I think everything's up for debate," McGinnis says.*

The Wilfrid Laurier University Faculty Association (WLUFA) joined in on the baseless accusations of heightened violence. The WLUFA President, Michele Kramer, wrote in a statement:[29]

> *To be clear, WLUFA condemns the violent speech and actions that have, unfortunately, become a daily occurrence on our campuses. In particular, the harm that has been leveled at our Trans Community and its supporters is unacceptable.*

Daily occurrences of violent speech and actions? If there was such a major uptick in criminal activity and assault, why weren't any police incidents being filed? Was it because the "violent speech and actions" were really things like critical emails and a few people giving the Rainbow Centre one-star ratings on Facebook? I had read a couple such Facebook reviews: "Not a very bright bunch of folks, they take offence to matters without understanding them, and make the rest of the trans community look bad," one said. "You do the community you claim to 'represent' a disservice," said another.

The College Fix, an online publication, reached out to Michele Kramer and asked her about what attacks were happening on campus. Kramer replied to them:[30]

> *While I appreciate your interest — and know that many people want these kinds of details — what we know for certain is that any time information has been given to the media throughout the course of this incident, threats against our members and others on campus have escalated.*
>
> *I cannot, in good conscience, supply any further information to you.*

What a winning tautological trick. First, claim that violent attacks and harassment are occurring on a daily basis on campus, then, when asked to specify what kinds of attacks are happening, claim that you cannot answer, as that would escalate the attacks that are happening.

The statement released by WLUFA also said "WLUFA stands in solidarity with our LGBTQ2 community as they continue to battle their way through walls of ignorance and oppression — walls that seem to have been disproportionately fortified in the last few weeks." WLUFA claimed that one of their main priorities was protecting "the physical, emotional and professional protection of our members — in the main, Drs. Rambukkana and Pimlott, but also certain members who have approached us with concerns regarding their emotional well-being and physical safety on campus."

On November 29, the Laurier undergraduate students' union and graduate students' union released a combined Letter from the Presidents (see full letter in Appendix C) reading:

> *We want to acknowledge that the events of last week, and the subsequent discourse associated with this topic, has caused harm for some Laurier students. The dominant narrative surrounding this story has too often discounted the lived experiences of transgender and non-binary students, and*

as a result, questioned their very existence… Educational engagement with
challenging material should not willfully incite hatred or violence.

Even the students' unions were suggesting a TVO clip was "challenging material" that incites hatred and violence, and that "discourse" can cause "harm." Unfortunately, their letter seemed to be representative of many students' views. In the November 29, 2017 edition of the Wilfrid Laurier student newspaper, The Cord, there was an extensive letter to the editor penned by the lengthy anonymous moniker, *"Concerned students of Wilfrid Laurier University who remain anonymous due to fear of harm, retribution, and repercussion. As the issue has been taken up in public discourse, L. Shepherd has been using their expanded public platform and social media following to target individuals and groups who have spoken out about the harm to the trans community. Students and resource support people at Laurier have been intentional targets of doxxing attacks by L. Shepherd, which has lead [sic] to ongoing intimidation, harassment, violence, and death threats."*[31]

In their letter, the Concerned Students wrote "we have recently reviewed the conversation regarding the problem of a Jordan Peterson (JP) video shown in a first-year class of undergraduate students, in the context of pronoun use, which, by the way, has nothing to do with the use of pronouns but everything to do with privilege, power, and oppression." They opined that showing the clip of The Agenda in class was "morally inexcusable," and proclaimed "L. Shepherd's tutorial was gendered violence perpetuated in class, as it is perpetuated in the wider school campus and in our province and country."

The Concerned Students said: "We have listened to both sides of the discussion per the audio recording, and we agree with the faculty and staff assessment – negating trans rights in the name of 'not taking sides' is against the Ontario Human Rights Code."

"JP's [Jordan Peterson's] rhetoric is not up for debate – it is hateful, spiteful, and violent and exudes a gendered white supremacist ideology."

"L. Shepherd departed from the goals of the tutorial by introducing the JP video and did so in a way that was detrimental to trans and non-binary students. If it [sic] not safe for students of marginalized status to come to a university for fear of being exposed to this type of discrimination and oppression, then will we continue to have student campuses populated by those of the dominant culture, that is cis-gender white people?" they wrote.

"As we are not members of the dominant population, we need to work double-hard to get where L. Shepherd is today."

They had to work "double-hard" to get where I am today, because I am a "cisgender white person"? How could they make such a shallow claim?

The remark reminded me of a speech I had heard the previous month at my convocation ceremony at SFU. I had flown back to BC to walk across the stage and formally receive my undergraduate degree. The honorary degree recipient presenting at the event was LGBTQ activist-author Ivan Coyote. In Ivan's speech, Ivan said:

> *I want you all to know, every single one of you, how proud I am of every single one of you today. Especially those of you who had to work harder, or longer, or come farther than the others did. My special love and admiration goes out today to anyone who was ever one of the only ones in their class. One of the few. One of the first. If you were ever one of the few women, one of the only queers in the room, the only immigrant, the only indigenous person, the only one sitting in a wheelchair, the first one ever in your family, the only one trying to find the gender-neutral washroom in your building, one of the few who had to translate the lecture or essay into or out of your mother tongue, then I want you to know that I know that you had to work harder and longer and come farther to be here today and I see you and I honour your achievements.*[32]

After Ivan's speech, all of the graduates around me applauded, but I did not. Someone who had to find a gender-neutral washroom in a building worked harder than everyone else? Ivan's speech negated all socioeconomic factors in favour of identity politics. Nay, not only socioeconomic factors, but all of the thousands of other factors that make up a human being. Students who were single parents to multiple kids trying to better their lives, or students facing financial hardship working 12-hour night shifts, or students who were battling addiction... they just didn't work as hard or come as far as indigenous people, immigrants, and queer people? Even if those indigenous people, immigrants or queer people came from wealthy, high-status, or well-connected families? Welcome to the "oppression olympics" that dominate university campuses. This is now the common view amongst the university arts-educated classes, that if you were "cisgender" and white, your life was just easier, and any socioeconomic circumstance or major life event you were facing could simply never compare to the circumstances of being an immigrant or not being heterosexual.

The Concerned Students' letter ended with a paragraph that read:

> *There is no room for white supremacy in a university setting, yet this situation is fraught with clear posturing of white supremacy. There is no room to use the guise of free speech/public debate/academic freedom to uphold white supremacy, yet white supremacy is defended. We are sorry Dr. MacLatchy, but your apology falls on the wrong side of right.*

What confused me about the Concerned Students' letter (aside from their insistence that somehow "white supremacy" played a huge part in this affair) was why these activists were claiming I had done something absolutely egregious by playing part of The Agenda in my tutorial, when to my knowledge, The Agenda itself – and its host Steve Paikin – had never had their studio protested or been subject to any petitions or open letters over their filming and airing of the episode. But when I aired a clip of a show that had already been on public, taxpayer-funded television, suddenly there was a problem.

An iconic Canadian weighed in with the same line of thought: Rick Mercer, famous for his short "Rick's Rants," dedicated his rant on November 29, 2017 to the Laurier controversy. It was titled "University Censorship:"[33]

> *They dragged a teaching assistant over the coals for the egregious crime of showing an interview in her classroom that had originally aired on public television. Now the idea being the students would watch the interview and then discuss the content. I know, it's a slippery slope… Next thing you know they'll be drowning kittens…*
>
> *I'm very glad that a so-called institute of higher learning is not charged with what I can, and cannot watch. If that was the case, I wouldn't have an opinion. I'd be ignorant, which I guess would make me the ideal student of the future. All universities should be paying very close attention to this, because the idea that young adults cannot be exposed to unpopular opinions in the classroom? That's an idea that's about as dangerous as an idea can get.*

The day after Rick's rant aired, I saw that one of my graduate student classmates had posted to Facebook, "Well Rick Mercer can fuck off. And I used to like him."

CHAPTER 10

It was December 1, 2017: the day I would be appearing on the Rubin Report. Classical liberal commentator Dave Rubin ran an extremely successful YouTube-based talk show featuring long-form interviews with guests like Ayaan Hirsi Ali, Sam Harris, and Jordan Peterson. I had arrived in California the night prior.

The morning before I was set to go live on the Rubin Report, I went down to the hotel restaurant and ordered avocado toast and a smoothie. Men in business suits were sitting back and chuckling amongst one another as they drank their morning coffees. Women in heels and sheath dresses tapped away furiously on their laptops. And here I was, among this professional class, in a Los Angeles hotel. I sat down at an empty table and opened my own laptop. I saw that a new episode of The Agenda with Steve Paikin had aired the night before.

The first segment of the episode was a panel discussion on the topic of free speech on campus, featuring five Ontarian academics as panelists. I figured I had enough time to watch the episode before I had to head to Dave Rubin's studio.

"The incidents at Wilfrid Laurier University have certainly provoked a debate within academia and beyond, on finding that sweet spot between freedom of expression and respecting the diversity of the student body. Is it possible to satisfy both of those legitimate aims? Let's find out," Steve Paikin announced as he introduced the episode.[34]

The five panelists engaged in a standard, ho-hum discussion of free speech, touching on the usual issues of safe spaces and trigger warnings. There was only one real stand-out moment on that show, in which University of Toronto professor Rinaldo Walcott stated:

> *Let's say his name, Professor Rambakooheh [sic], found himself in a very difficult situation, he's an untenured man of colour. I know that as a young,*

untenured black professor, when I had white TAs, they often felt that they could do the course better than I could, too. And they often overstretched their own responsibilities as TAs. I am sure that in the context of this one particular instance that there's much more surrounding that professor's own experience with this young white woman.

A sentiment I had become somewhat used to by now washed over me: annoyance at someone reading their own agenda into events they knew nothing about. Walcott was claiming there was so much more to the story in regard to me and Rambukkana's working relationship, when the truth was, I had barely interacted with the man. We mainly communicated with the occasional email, and when we did communicate, I always took his direction. There was only one issue that had come up in the past, when Rambukkana ordered me to artificially lower a high-achieving student's grade because he didn't want anyone to receive a perfect score. I sent him one email laying out the reasons why I thought the student truly deserved an A+, but he rejected my plea and told me that getting an A+ should be impossible on the annotated bibliography assignment. I obeyed him and lowered the girl's grade.

Why did Walcott think it was appropriate to make such a conjecture on public television, that I was stepping over my boundaries as a TA because my supervisor was not white? And besides: Pimlott was a white professor and had been included in my recording, why wasn't Walcott reading into the racial dynamic of the white student subverting her white MA coordinator?

Walcott doubled down on the comments he made during The Agenda, later tweeting, "I have not work [sic] with Teaching Assistants for many years. I teach mainly grad students or upper level courses. BIPOC [Black, Indigenous, People of Colour] professors should start a hashtag something like #whatmywhiteTAdidtome because many of us know some of our white TAs attempt to undermine our authority as profs."[35]

According to Walcott, if your course supervisor happens to be non-white, they should not be called out on any wrongdoing. If a non-white professor invents complaints against you to try to make you toe an ideological line, you should spare them of being called out on their abuse of power, because they're not white.

Walcott wasn't the only professor on the panel who had an issue with me: Shannon Dea of the University of Waterloo stated that in the inquisition, Rambukkana, Pimlott and Joel were simply trying to offer me feedback on my "bad pedagogy."

"I happened to think the pedagogy was bad... I think that given the intended learning outcomes for that class, it was bad pedagogy."

I knew by now that if someone in an academic position fails to transmit the approved leftist ideology to students, they have "bad pedagogy."

I clicked on the second segment of that episode of The Agenda, featuring none other than Laurier president Deborah MacLatchy. The president of Laurier, on The Agenda, discussing the incident where I had been reprimanded over showing a clip from The Agenda, at Laurier. It was all so meta.

Steve Paikin's first question to MacLatchy was, "In your view, did Lindsay Shepherd do anything wrong?"[36]

MacLatchy began, "I think I'd just like to start by just saying this really is an unfortunate incident that has brought a really important discussion to the forefront, not only for universities but for the broader public as well. I can't speak to what happened in the classroom because I wasn't there."

She continued: "I think really, the discussion really about what happens in the classroom is not just only about the material that is presented, but how it's presented... that includes ensuring that material that's presented is evidence-based that it's been critically reviewed that it's been analyzed that in a way that when it's presented and discussed with the students, that they understand what the scholarly underpinning is."

"Did Lindsay fail that test?" asked Paikin.

"I don't know what happened in that classroom, and so that is why the university is undertaking a third-party fact-finding activity in order to better understand what happened in the classroom," replied MacLatchy.

Steve Paikin then questioned whether Laurier is living up to its stated commitment to free expression, as the university had recently posted a video on YouTube titled "Laurier President discusses university's century-old commitment to freedom of expression," where MacLatchy said a few platitudinal words about how freedom of expression is important, but hate and intolerance are bad.

"Don't know, again, because I wasn't in the classroom..." she responded to Paikin.

"But you know what happened..." Paikin began. He was cut off by MacLatchy, who started talking about how discussions in the classroom must not be uncivil or intolerant, and they should not violate human rights or demean students.

"Do you have any reason to believe any of that happened here?" countered Paikin.

"Don't know what happened in the classroom," MacLatchy said with a smirk. She also had the gall to giggle, as if it were somehow funny that she could only parrot lines that the university PR team fed to her. She was really working for her $350,000 annual salary.

"M'kay, I'm gonna skip the next three questions then, because they're kind of along that line," said Paikin.

I wished Paikin had pushed her a bit more. Watching MacLatchy in that interview, I pitied her, in a way: when I made media appearances, I could express exactly what I thought. I could be honest and authentic. There was a freedom that comes with only representing yourself and no one else – you don't risk facing backlash from any donor, boss, or overlord. MacLatchy was forced to stick to a script conjured up by her media and PR team; her humanity taken away by bureaucracy. Whether she privately supported me or privately supported the free speech detractors didn't matter – it was sad that she was not permitted to express any of her own thoughts.

I closed my laptop and called an Uber – I had to be at Dave Rubin's studio in ten minutes.

CHAPTER 11

I arrived back in Waterloo after my 24-hour trip to LA, happy to be receiving an influx of supportive messages from people who had seen me on the Rubin Report. But the students and professors of Wilfrid Laurier University were still living in a state of terror. They had now begun demanding panic buttons and bulletproof windows.

An undistinguished Communication Studies professor named Jeremy Hunsinger wrote on Twitter, "I am somewhat disturbed by the news that several of my colleagues have panic buttons in their offices...I get it..."[37]

On December 1, 2017, the Rainbow Centre issued a list of demands on Facebook.[38] One of the demands stated "President Deb MacLatchy must issue a public apology to trans, non-binary, and gender diverse students, staff, and faculty, for failing to acknowledge the transphobia that exists on our campus or provide adequate supports. We want you to say that you are sorry for failing to uphold the experiences and safety of trans, non-binary, and gender diverse people in the Laurier community and for your complicity in maintaining transphobia. #sayitDeb."

Next, the Rainbow Centre demanded that the university "immediately implement safety measures that have already been requested by the Rainbow Centre, including the installation of a panic button and reinforced windows in all DEO [Diversity & Equity Office] centres and offices. Create proactive safety processes in consultation with all members of the Diversity & Equity Office so that future safety concerns can be addressed immediately when threats to marginalized students occur."

The proceeding items in the Rainbow Centre's list requested jobs, money, and resources.

"Hire a second full-time Sexual Violence Response Coordinator within the Diversity & Equity Office in order to help respond to the experiences of gender-based violence that are occurring on campus. This demand will increase the availability of supports to survivors of transphobia and all other forms of gender-based violence within an office that is grossly overworked and understaffed."

"Hire a trans person of colour as a full-time counsellor within the Diversity & Equity Office to provide mental health supports to individuals who are being impacted by our campus climate."

"Establish a fund of at least $5000.00 per year that can be accessed by all departments at Laurier so that faculty, staff, and teaching assistants can access trans education workshops and pay trans and non-binary facilitators."

"Hire a trans faculty member to serve as a Canadian Research Chair on transphobia in post-secondary educational institutions. This individual will conduct research on institutionalized transphobia at Laurier and provide recommendations for policies and procedures that promote gender equity and support trans, non-binary, and gender diverse students, staff, and faculty."

I wondered how sincere the Rainbow Centre affiliates were being about all of the harm and hurt they were facing, because, again, they never substantiated their claims of rampant harassment. It seemed to me that they saw an opportunity in the Laurier controversy to secure university resources for themselves to advance their political ideologies.

When the announcement of the Laurier task force had been made the week prior, a Rainbow Centre affiliate took to social media to ask what resources and funding they would be given.

"Wilfrid Laurier University why are you proposing a free speech task force without adequately providing compensation or resources for marginalized bodies?" the Communication Studies graduate student wrote. I screenshotted his reply and tweeted, cheekily, "It all makes sense now. This is why affiliates of the WLU Rainbow Centre are relentlessly insisting that I have caused them harm and that they are actually at the centre of a free speech issue. They want…compensation. $$$."[39]

I thought the graduate student's tweet was an instructive comment: why did these people think they deserved money just because other people wanted to partake in open discussions? As Jonathan Rauch wrote in Kindly Inquisitors, "people who are 'hurt by words' are morally entitled to nothing whatsoever by way of compensation," and the response to people asking for such things should effectively be "too bad, so sad."

Little did I know that publicly replying to this particular grad student's tweet would get me in trouble a few months later. But I won't get ahead of myself.

*

After the Rainbow Centre released their demands for jobs and money, new posters were plastered around the campus, featuring the hashtags "#Nametransphobia" and "#SayItDeb." These posters were a hot item in the Communication Studies hallway: almost every professor had one on their office door.

On December 5, a group of professors sent out yet another open letter:[40]

> *Dear Wilfrid Laurier University Administration,*
>
> *We are Wilfrid Laurier University faculty members who are troubled by the events that have recently taken place on our campus, the mishandling of these events, and the impacts on trans, non-binary, and gender diverse students, staff, and faculty, [sic]*
>
> *We call on the administration to immediately:*

119

1. Name transphobia

Up to this point, the administration has willfully refused to name transphobia as a problem at our institution, in the harassment against students, staff, and faculty, and as a broader problem in our society.

By not-naming the problem, the administration has been complicit in perpetuating this issue.

2. Issue a public apology to transgender, non-binary and gender diverse students, staff and faculty for refusing to acknowledge how these events have perpetuated transphobia in our institution.

3. Take meaningful steps to ensure the safety of staff at the Rainbow Center [sic] and Diversity and Equity Office

Despite the administration's public claims, we are not convinced that the university has dedicated enough time, resources, or even careful thought into ensuring the safety of these offices.

Since the university's actions have been insufficient, a group of concerned faculty and staff has taken this issue up and organized a rota to ensure that there is least one member of faculty present in these offices during their open hours. However, this is not a permanent solution: the university needs to take action to ensure that the Rainbow Centre and DEO remain safe spaces.

4. Postpone the creation of the taskforce until proper consultation has been implemented

The pace at which the task force is progressing is too rushed.

We need to reflect upon the mandate, purpose and composition of this task force, and indeed, if it reflects the needs of the broader community.

Retraumatisation and fear of repercussions are significant barriers for many of the faculty that have been directly impacted by this event. The process of publicizing names of nominees leaves them potentially vulnerable in this climate. We are also concerned that our university is not yet in a position to undertake an initiative of this kind, given the divisiveness of the issues and safety concerns raised.

Instead of rushing to define the issue solely as freedom of expression, the university needs to develop a more inclusive and robust model for addressing freedom expression that is balanced with human rights.

This is a tremendous opportunity for our university and we should take some time pause, reflect and then develop a more informed strategy for tackling this issue.

5. WLU needs to develop an equity and diversity statement that acts as the framework that guides the rest of this process.

We need to strike up a committee composed of experts in the areas of gender-based violence, transphobia and other forms of systemic violence, many of whom are already working at our institution, to develop this policy. This policy will provide a framework for creating a more just and inclusive campus.

This initiative should be distinct from the "Task Force".

6. A formal inquiry must be launched to examine how the upper administration mishandled the public relations surrounding the situation, which has led to heightened risks for students, staff and faculty.

In responding to original media coverage, the administration has made many missteps – including quick, reactive and non-consultative actions such as the creation of the Task Force - and many members of the Laurier community have been negatively impacted as a result. We need to examine how these decisions were made so that we can improve as an institution moving forward and not make the same mistakes again.

We the undersigned faculty support the needs articulated by the transgender, non-binary, and gender diverse students at Wilfrid Laurier University.

The letter was signed by 30 faculty members, from the departments of Sociology, Global Studies, English, and the like. No professor from any kind of math, business, or science department signed on.

By now, it should be more than obvious to you, reader, that I was not particularly liked by many faculty members at my university. There was a constant nagging at the back of my mind throughout these weeks: I had to secure an MA supervisor from within the CAST department by mid-December if I was going to proceed with the major research paper stream of my degree instead of defaulting to the course-based option. I had an ally in Dr. Haskell, but he was from outside my home department, and could only serve as the second reader and not the main supervisor. The deadline to find a supervisor was fast-approaching.

Someone told me about a Facebook group where professors discussed academia-related news, called "Take Academia Back!" A Communication Studies professor affiliated with the MA CAST department, Dr. Penelope Ironstone, was a co-founder of the page. I would see articles about me and the Laurier controversy being posted on the page, but only articles that disparaged me – and I would see that some professors in my department, such as Dr. Ironstone, would "Like" those articles. These professors were openly indicating what they thought about me, but in the most underhanded manner, so that they couldn't be accused of taking any overt stance. I would sound petty if I were to complain that "some of my professors liked mean articles about me on Facebook." Even the official Laurier Sociology department Twitter account was liking tweets that mocked me.

Resigned, I figured I would have to do the coursework-based stream and not write a major research paper, as I was too daunted by the prospect of finding a potential supervisor when it seemed like they all hated me. I was disappointed: I had wanted to challenge myself by taking on a 50-page paper, to prove to myself that I could do it – but figured it just wasn't going to work out.

It wasn't only professors from within Laurier who were open about expressing their contempt for me – professors at neighbouring universities were writing about me on their blogs as well. Aimée Morrison, an Associate Professor of English at the University of Waterloo, wrote in her feminism-themed blog (tagline: "Fast feminism. Slow academe") that the whole gist of the Laurier affair was much ado over a "bad teaching decision."[41] Morrison said it was "bullshit" that controversial speech on campus might be chilled following the Laurier affair.

Morrison wrote about my "canny deployment of White Lady Tears (TM)," and said I am

> *...absolutely, 100% running circles around administrators and professors of all sorts who somehow cannot frame a response to this that doesn't advance an anti-intellectual, transphobic, misogynistic, white supremacist alt-right agenda. It's an amaaaaaaaazing degree of incompetence. She doesn't seem to be terribly smart, but my god, is she clever. And she's totally winning at this in ways that make all of us lose.*

I don't "seem to be terribly smart"? What encouraging words for a graduate student to hear from a local professor at the neighbouring university.

She concluded:

> *Progressive academics, we need to get clever. The battle for hearts and minds on Twitter and in the op-ed pages moves fast, and the agenda is being set by the alt-right. We need to get serious about learning how to effectively engage on these platforms, and fast. Because from what I'm watching, never have such a collection of highly educated and possibly even well meaning people undermined their own careers, scholarship, and values so quickly and effectively as they have these week, and made themselves look stupid losing a public relations battle to a 22 year old alt-right provocateur.*

She took one last shot before signing off, calling me an "out-of-line, intellectually nonsensical MA student."

Other professors were mentioning me in podcasts and giving academic presentations about my case at conferences: A Publishing professor at my alma mater of SFU, Hannah McGregor, had a podcast called "Secret Feminist Agenda,"[42] and in one episode she spouted off a list of "shitty white women" that included two authors – Angie Abdou and the legendary Margaret Atwood – and little old me.

McGregor also presented at Congress, one of Canada's largest conferences of the arts and social sciences, and her presentation write-up read:

> *Over the past year conversations about free speech on university campuses have been receiving an unprecedented level of mainstream media coverage. In Canada, this coverage has centred around controversial figures such as Jordan Peterson and Lindsay Shepherd and have, in often unsettling ways, focused on their extremist positions over attention to how universities actually function… This presentation thinks through what it would look like to make the work of the university more public, and whether that might fight against the disinformation of extremist positions.*[43]

It was stuff like this that reminded me why I had gone public with my recording: it provided people with a raw look inside the university. What happens in the sphere of academia is mostly unknown to outsiders – all I can see from the conference write-up that a presentation occurred based on the premise that I was an extremist. Other than that, I have no idea what conference attendees heard.

Postsecondary education consultant Alex Usher defended my use of the TVO clip in class, commenting that in the clip "Peterson is doing his usual irritating mixture of belligerent arrogance and victimhood, but if the purpose of the exercise was to examine the question 'how does language evolve'/ 'how do politics affect the evolution of language' it's not a terrible clip to play. It's not 'hate', as some people would have it."[44] Usher continued, though, by stating, "that said, Shepherd can't be all that bright if she genuinely thought that playing this clip wouldn't trigger a reaction."

I felt defeated. I had been excited at the chance to discuss a topical issue with my undergraduate students, who I regarded as mature individuals capable of sharing their thoughts without breaking down into hysterics (which, they were, and they didn't) – but everyone around me was acting like universities were no such place to discuss topics of social currency, between Rambukkana saying the students were "too young" for Peterson's ideas and Usher lending credence to the notion that university students were triggered individuals who were incapable of being intellectual curious. It was all so disappointing. Even my fellow TAs referred to the undergraduate students as "children" and "kids" during our meetings. I wonder if my TAs and professors referred to me as a "child" or "kid" when I was an undergraduate student. How did we let universities slip into being thought of as day camps?

All you get for treating your students like capable and curious adults, and wanting to instill a sense of intellectual maturity in them, is the "experts" like Usher and Morrison ridiculing you and insulting your intelligence. Fortunately, a University of Waterloo professor named James Skidmore pushed back against Usher, commenting:

> *I'm astounded that so many people, on the basis of incomplete information about the class in question, are so quick to judge Ms. Shepherd's ability as an instructor. No university instructor would welcome the conjecture surrounding their teaching practices based on their choice of materials.*

> *You might think Ms. Shepherd's not too bright, but how bright are you for assuming what actually occurred in the class on the basis of one clip that was shown? We know nothing about the rest of that period – how Ms. Shepherd handled questions, what the students said about the video, etc. What we do know is that a student in the class complained, that Ms. Shepherd was subjected to a process by two profs and one administrator that was unprofessional at best, that Ms. Shepherd taped that conversation without their knowledge, that the university has apologized to Ms. Shepherd for how the matter was handled, as has one of the three people who met with her in the first place (though the other two have not). Talk about that process and those facts all you want.*

But resist the urge to provide free teaching advice. Your suggestion is for Ms. Shepherd to find a clip that can present the ideas of Peterson without using Peterson, because some students will have an automatic reaction towards this man whom they dislike so much. I teach courses on Nazi Germany, and I'm glad you haven't seen some of the clips I've played – you might assume I lack enough imagination to find less "triggering" clips and start providing me with suggestions about how to discuss Hitler and his ideas without showing clips of the man or having students read some of his writing. (By the way, regardless of how well I prepare and present those materials, I can't control the reactions of the students. I can only hope they'll come to talk to me about it first instead of heading straight for a university administrator.)

Another professor wrote in defense of me: Paul Adams, an associate professor of journalism at the University of Manitoba, said in iPolitics:[45]

Shepherd recorded the exchange — which brings me to the second striking thing about it: how hopelessly inept these academics were at managing a serious conversation about a difficult subject, compared with Paikin's careful stewardship.

The things they said.

Rambukkana briefly hesitates to compare Peterson to Hitler — then plunges right in and does it anyway. The other professor repeatedly mixes up J. Philippe Rushton (a one-time professor at Western University, now dead, who argued that races have different levels of intelligence, sexual restraint and inclination to obey the law) with Charles Murray — the American political scientist (still alive) who continues to argue that America's social strata reflect different levels of intelligence rather than social conditions. A racist is a racist, I guess.

The same professor (or so it seems from the recording) dismissively refers to Paikin's hour-long program as a "YouTube video" and later pipes up cluelessly: "Is grammar not something that's really not subject to debate?"

126

*They sound, well, like people who are used to standing up in front of a class
and talking for a long time without being challenged or interrupted — an
experience which is not good for the soul.*

I was always so grateful for such comments. I would say "Thank you" to
them aloud. They were so reasonable. So sensical. So beautiful.

*

On December 7, 2017 it was my 23rd birthday, and my friend Sophie,
who was completing her MA in Environmental Policy at Memorial
University in Newfoundland, was making a stop in Waterloo for a couple
nights before flying back home to BC for the holidays. It was the last
week of classes, so Sophie waited in the library as I attended my last
graduate class of the semester, the theme being intersectional feminism.
The presenting student lectured about the work of critical race theorist
Kimberlé Crenshaw, the professor who coined the term
"intersectionality" as a way to describe how race, gender, ability, and class
intersect to form one's identity.

The presenting student then showed a short video on-screen of a black
woman slowly unravelling an Islamic headscarf as she looked straight into
the camera. In the final shot, the woman revealed dreadlocked hair. The
presenting student addressed the class: "Why did I show you this video?"

The class was quiet. A few people raised their hands and gave
nonsensical, irrelevant answers.

I raised my hand, as it was getting painful. The presenter stiffened: I was
the only one with my hand up, so he knew he had to call on me. His
reluctance was tangible. "Lindsay?" he said, with the slightest little sigh.

"This video portrays an intersectional identity, as not only is this woman
black, with the culturally black hairstyle of dreadlocks, but she is also a
Muslim, as shown by her hijab."

127

The presenter almost looked surprised at my answer, even though this was a middle-school level analysis. "Yes, that's right," he said.

I glanced over at the professor, Dr. Ironstone, who was staring ahead with an irritated look on her face.

After class, Sophie and I boarded the Greyhound to Toronto, and spent my birthday browsing the Royal Ontario Museum. I remember having to do a scheduled radio interview that day, and desperately looking for a private area in the museum to do the call, before settling on the floor of a semi-quiet hallway.

I also spoke on the phone with Howard Levitt, my lawyer. He had important information to share: the previous weekend, he had written an email to the third-party investigator hired by Laurier, Rob Centa, asking for the details about the complaint or complaints made against me.

Rob Centa replied, "I do not believe there is a document that contains a 'complaint' made about Ms. Shepherd nor is there anything I would describe as a formal complaint under any WLU policy."

The plot was thickening.

*

While I was in Toronto, back on the Wilfrid Laurier campus the Rainbow Centre had organized a Trans Solidarity Rally in the quad area outside of the student centre, with approximately 80 people in attendance.[46] I watched a video of the rally, as I couldn't be there in person.

A Laurier PhD student named Kira Williams was one of the rally speakers. Williams cried "Fuck Lindsay Shepherd" and claimed to the audience that I had violated the Ontario Human Rights Code and violated "the spirit of the Charter of Rights and Freedoms" by playing hate speech in the classroom – "hate speech that says people like me, like you [trans people] should not exist in the classroom, literally."

Prior to the Laurier affair, I was somewhat starstruck when I heard someone was a PhD student: I automatically thought they must be an exceptionally wise, disciplined, and rational person. Now I knew that if you are the right kind of activist, getting into graduate-level arts programs is actually very easy, and certainly does not require any wisdom – nor will graduates have gained any wisdom after their years of attaining their degree.

"The board of governors… They don't give a shit," said Williams. "We not only deserve an apology, but we deserve to hear the university recognize our fucking existence, 'cause we exist."

"Dr. Peterson is a transphobic hack," Williams continued. "Having his words in the classroom causes violence against others… so what I was really fucking pissed about is that again, there was no apology, there wasn't even a mention that we exist! And of course, we do."[47]

It was more of the same: their existence was being denied, their lives were not up for debate, speech is violence, and everyone needed to apologize to them.

Another graduate student, Ethan Jackson, took his place on the stage during the rally. Ethan said, in a mock-hushed voice, that "violence is okay"[48] as a means of fighting transphobia, and that "you can see the fear" in President Deb MacLatchy's eyes when she is confronted by the trans activists – adding, "she should be scared. There's so much she should be scared of, because we have so much power and resistance."

When I jumped onto Twitter later that day, I noticed that Ethan had tweeted at me: "@NewWorldHominin why weren't you at the Trans Justice Rally today if you so boldly deny your participation in causing trans/gender variant & NB [non-binary] folx harm? What are your priorities?"

I tweeted back at him saying I had other plans that day because it was my birthday, but "I know, I know…you and your identity should always come first!"

The following week, Ethan tweeted at me again, saying "@NewWorldHominin Where did you learn how to use social media; who gave you all of your skills, mechanisms, lines and scripts to use social media in this grandiose capacity for someone (you boo) who never had social media, 0 profiles, or used social media before. Seems suspicious."

I replied to him by calling him a conspiracy theorist. Many people were convinced someone was orchestrating everything I was doing throughout the Laurier controversy; providing me with a script and puppeteering me. Some anonymous Twitter users maintained that it was Jordan Peterson doing the puppeteering, even though the extent of my and Jordan Peterson's communication was a couple of brief email exchanges.

But the boring old truth was that I was very much on my own and left to my own devices. At most, I would show a tweet to my mom and ask her if she thought it was a good thing to post – that was the extent of my PR strategy.

National Post columnist Barbara Kay was one of the people who replied to Ethan on Twitter, saying, "learning Twitter is not rocket science. Did you find it difficult? I am 75 and learned the ins and outs of it in a few days. Wanna tutorial?"[49]

I did a quick Google search of Ethan to get a sense of what his deal was, and why he kept directing tweets at me. It turns out he had a history of opposing freedom of expression: in 2013, he had dressed up in a costume of a giant vulva and protested a pro-life speech by a local Conservative MP at the time, Stephen Woodworth, on the University of Waterloo campus. He and the other protesters were meshing with police, as one of the activists cried, "You are threatening the freedom of all cunts and disseminating anti-cunt misinformation," along with chants of "Shame!" Woodworth packed up and left without delivering his presentation, and the activists cheered when Woodworth exited the room.[50]

"Aren't you the person who dressed up in a genitalia costume and effectively shut down a talk by an MP at UWaterloo?" I tweeted back at Ethan. It was all good fun.

*

I was waiting in line at the Greyhound station in Toronto, waiting for my bus back to Waterloo after a podcast interview, when I got a text from a friend: "The Maclean's article is out!" I clicked the link to the piece: "What really happened at Wilfrid Laurier University: Inside Lindsay Shepherd's heroic, insulting, brave, destructive, possibly naïve fight for free speech." One particular section of the article piqued my interest, where the reporter, Aaron Hutchins, outlined his attempts to connect with the Communication Studies faculty:

> *Among Laurier's communications studies faculty, many aren't willing to talk about what's happening on campus. At least not on the record with the media.*

> *When reached by phone by Maclean's, Rambukkana immediately hung up. Via email he said he was advised by his union not to speak with reporters. After he declined to comment, Maclean's was contacted by several communications studies students and faculty.*

> *(In a follow up email, Rambukkana writes: "I did not contact any students to suggest that they speak to you, or any members of the media, regarding this issue. After you had been in contact with some students and colleagues, some students spoke to me about their contact with you." He did, however, forward the media request on to colleagues, who in turn forwarded the request to*

students. Several faculty members and students reached out and asked to comment via questions over email and under the condition of anonymity—both requests were denied and interviews never took place.)

Those who do speak are being extra careful with their words. In a telephone interview with Maclean's, Laurier student Vivek Ramesh answers questions as voices in the background—who are never named—can be heard whispering responses to him.

In a follow-up interview the next day, there are no whisperers in the background, but Ramesh's criticism of Shepherd remains. "If we do anything as TAs to alienate any students, we've failed in our job as a TA and our duties in these entry-level communications courses," he says. "We're there to help to level the playing field in terms of writing. We're not there to generate controversial discussion and do any deep-dive critical thinking. That's what upper-year courses are for."

Ramesh says the larger issue is a lack of guidance for TAs from professors. "In order to generate interest—because grammar is a boring topic—[other TAs] were doing things like dissecting celebrity tweets and fixing the grammar and structure," he says. "The kind of content [Shepherd] brought in was definitely inappropriate. [...] At no point should your discussion devolve into should gender fluid and trans people's identity come into question."

Hutchins' article exposed an underbelly of the Communication Studies department that I hadn't known. It was all so creepy and cult-like, between the graduate student, Vivek Ramesh, having voices whisper responses to him in the background as he spoke to the media, and Rambukkana hanging up on the reporter but circulating media requests to his allies in the department. And how sad that Ramesh had really said that TAs aren't there to "do any deep-dive critical thinking." Critical thinking isn't something you turn on and off; it is integrated into your everyday existence.

Kira Williams, the PhD student who spoke at the Trans Solidarity Rally, had found their way into the Maclean's article as well:

> Kira Williams experiences something transphobic every day. Some days that's harassment. Other days it's sexual assault. "The reality is Dr. Peterson's speech is targeted at trans people," says the Laurier PhD student. "And the reality is that when people like Peterson speak, it has consequences in the real world—consequences I have to live through every day."

Ah yes, sexual assault, just something I experience every other day or so. Some days it's harassment, some days it's sexual assault.

Why did these activists always make claims that could never be substantiated? Why were they so flippant about their use of serious terms reserved for criminal behaviour, like hate speech and sexual assault?

*

In mid-December, yet another open letter was circulating: this time, a letter signed off by the majority of the Wilfrid Laurier Communication Studies faculty, distributed to the entire email list of the Canadian Communication Association (see full letter in Appendix D).

"Public debates about freedom of expression, while valuable, can have a silencing effect on the free speech of other members of the public," the letter said.

"We are always so grateful when students do approach campus offices designed for reporting problematic classroom situations, as their courage makes us do our jobs better. We thank you for coming forward: you are such valued members of our community."

It then said, laughably, "Charges that our program shelters students from real-world issues or fosters classrooms inhospitable to discussing

133

contentious issues from different vantage points seem to us simply preposterous."

The letter called for better "training" of TAs (read: better monitoring to ensure TAs will instill the approved leftist viewpoints in students). Similarly, the letter said that controversial issues in the classroom need "pedagogical care."

By then, I was accustomed to people claiming that there was no way a 22-year old Master's student was able to handle such a sensitive and fraught topic such as gender pronouns with the proper "care"– as a 22-year old graduate student would not have the necessary "teaching skills." This was all empty condescension. It was like when Rambukkana claimed 18-year olds were not able to process Peterson's viewpoints. These arrogant academics thought young people had to be trained, educated, and "given the tools" to understand the approved leftist worldview. Openness to new or different ideas is not tolerated: anyone exposing you to different ideas doesn't know how to teach, lacks experience, and has bad pedagogy. Surely, if I had played the exact same TVO clip for my class, but talked about how transphobic Jordan Peterson was, I would be lauded for my strong teaching skills and excellent pedagogy, and probably would have won a teaching award.

The letter concluded:

> *Commentary on this event in the press and social media has emboldened individuals who see themselves as noble defenders of free speech to intimidate our faculty and students — to the point that protective measures have been taken in an attempt to secure their safety. Against this politics of revenge, we acknowledge the moral imperative to support and protect our colleagues and students.*

The undersigned were almost everyone in the Communication Studies department, save a handful of names.

But one particular name stood out to me from the list: Judith Nicholson. I had known since the start of the academic year that Nicholson would be teaching Communication Studies 101 in the January–April 2018 term: she would be my next supervisor, taking over for Rambukkana. I sighed, knowing that my supervisor for the next term had already made up her mind about what was going on. I completely supported her right to sign whatever letters she wished, and for her to advocate for whatever causes she wanted to. But I knew I would have to watch my back the next semester. Maybe it's good that she gave me the warning.

Fortunately, one professor in the MA CAST program was making a positive impact on my degree: before the end of the semester, I received an out-of-the-blue email from Dr. Milo Sweedler.

> *Hi Lindsay,*
>
> *Just a quick word to touch base and see how you are doing. I cannot imagine what you have been going through these past few weeks. If you have a minute to breathe and want to talk, please do not hesitate to stop by my office, send me an email or give a call. It would be a pleasure.*
>
> *Otherwise, on a tangential note, it strikes me that you have one hell of an MRP topic if you want to pursue it. I would be happy to supervise or act as a second reader of your MRP if you want to delve into the issues that your case has brought to the surface. It would be a fascinating topic to pursue, and no one is better placed to pursue it than you.*
>
> *I hope that you are hanging in there.*

It was a miracle. A professor from my department was offering to be my MA supervisor. I would now be able to complete my degree the way I had always wanted to, and a topic had fallen right into my lap. When I met with Prof. Sweedler in his office, he said that he was "ambivalent" about the Laurier controversy. Good enough for me!

Prof. Haskell agreed to be my second reader, and just like that, I could continue on at Laurier and write the major research paper as originally planned.

CHAPTER 12

The end of the Fall 2017 semester was nearing. I had a flight booked to go home to BC for the Christmas holidays once I had no more classes or meetings to attend.

As I was boarding the bus to the Laurier campus on one of the last days I had to be there, I glanced at the clear container of newspapers for sale that was displayed at the front of the vehicle. I did a double take: I saw my own curled brown hair and pink jacket in the photo featured on the cover page. "Who is Lindsay Shepherd?" read the headline of the December 12, 2017 edition of the Waterloo Region Record. I knew one of their reporters was writing a profile on me, but I didn't know it would be the front page story! I took one of the newspapers out of the plastic box and scrounged up one dollar in change from my wallet.

"I'll get one of those papers," I said, handing the change over to the bus driver, and tucking my newspaper away.

I thought of the day the front page photo of me was taken, when I met the photographer underneath the stairs outside the library in a quiet area with some tables and mural art. There were also some windows at ground level which belonged to the library's staff-only areas.

During the photoshoot, I was trying to pay attention to the photographer's directions, but I could see from the corner of my eye a man taking a photo of me on his cell phone from the inside of the library's staff area – his phone pressed right up to the window. After he took the pictures, he retreated back into the staff room, shutting the blinds.

A week later, I found out that that man was a Laurier librarian, Matt Thomas. He had posted the picture he took on Twitter. He wrote a snarky little comment with his post: "Ah, I thought it looked like Lindsay

Shepherd...She's really taking advantage of the publicity. Shame she has so little freedom of speech."[51]

It was slightly unsettling that a Wilfrid Laurier University staff member – a librarian – thought it was appropriate to sneak a photo of me, post it to his social media account, and make some sort of bad faith comment implying I was a fame whore for accepting a media request. It was strange because I did not occupy a space of being a recognizable celebrity who could expect people to be taking photos of me: I was just a graduate student, not a famous person. I suppose all notions of professional and respectful behavior towards an institution's students disappear if you don't like the student's politics or worldview.

*

I was sitting at my mom's dining room table in Coquitlam, BC working on a class assignment due in mid-December as CBC radio played in the background. CBC radio was always on in the background of my mom's house. I was tapping away on my laptop, tuning out the noise, but my ears perked up when I thought I heard the word "teaching assistant" in a discussion of 2017's top stories.

"Jesse, what about for you, are there stories you thought got too much coverage, stories that you'd be very happy to never hear anything about again?" the radio host asked Jesse Wente, a pundit and indigenous activist.[52]

"...anything with a teaching assistant?" he answered to the amusement of the panel, who all snickered.

"Oh god, I never want to hear the name Lindsay Shepherd ever again!" Tabatha Southey said as the panel cackled.

"Tabatha, was there anything you think got too much coverage in 2017?"

"Nope, just Lindsay Shepherd, that's it." They continued laughing.

I turned my head back towards my laptop and resumed writing my paper. It was strange to be externally encountered with yourself when you are going about your day. After being steeped in a national controversy for a few weeks, reading article after article about myself and reviewing my media appearances, I felt like I was being forced to think about myself too much, when I would usually be thinking about other things.

That CBC radio program I heard in my mom's kitchen wasn't the only one that had mentioned me in their year-in-review programming: on the CBC News Network Sunday Scrum from December 17, 2017, journalist John Ibbitson named me as a 2017 newsmaker of the year.[53] It was only an informal acknowledgment, but it felt like an honour to me.

However, one panelist, a writer named Vicky Mochama, countered Ibbitson's nomination.

"I have to disagree," said Mochama. "I think that she is someone that exists, and I think a lot of people responded to her for the same reasons they tend to respond to things, which is that she's a young, crying white girl… I don't think that she's the appropriate person to have launched this conversation because as it turns out she leans hard right in some of her choices."

How nice of her to acknowledge that I am "someone that exists." Maybe the trans activists were onto something, in their demands for others to acknowledge their existence!

"Well, whether you like where she leans or not, we're having this debate here on this show now and we're having it because of Ms. Shepherd," Ibbitson replied, to which a visibly annoyed Mochama twitchily pursed her lips and squinted her eyes.

139

I watched the clip a second and third time to ensure I had heard everything accurately. I was nothing more than a "crying white girl," and I'm not the right person to have launched this conversation because I apparently lean "hard right in some of [my] choices?"

Don't get me wrong: I absolutely believed that Mochama should be permitted to express her views, and I would never advocate for her to be censored or removed from her pundit position. But the message here was clear: she was dismissing the issues of the Laurier affair because of my skin colour, and she was dismissing the issues of open inquiry and the pursuit of truth within the university because she construed me as "hard right" (she, of course, never indicated in what ways I was "hard right"). Apparently, because I am not a radical leftist, that invalidated all of the issues I had brought to light.

Another CBC panelist, Susan Riley, added "I do think she's being co-opted, or at least – I don't know where she started on the ideological spectrum, she says she was on the left but she's definitely being used now by the right."

While Susan seemed to be more or less sympathetic to my plight, I had grown weary of claims that I was being used and co-opted. It robbed me of my agency, and it was condescending. Yes, right-wingers and conservatives were drawn to my story. Did that nullify the legitimacy of my case? There seemed to be some sort of Leftists' Law: as soon as a right-winger is drawn to something, that thing becomes contemptible.

After Mochama called me a crying white girl, others gleefully echoed her words. Rinaldo Walcott, the professor who accused me of purposely undermining Rambukkana's authority for the sole reason that Rambukkana is not white, tweeted "Crying white girl crys [sic] about being called crying white girl. Will the defenders get their guns, nooses, baseball bats among their other weapons to inflict violence now?"[54]

A PhD student at York University wrote an essay called "The Crying White Girl: Lindsay Shepherd, Victimhood and White Positionalities."[55] He wrote that his paper would examine:

> ...how Shepherd's use of the crying white girl digital trope places her within a series of racial relations where white victimhood is constructed at the expense of minoritarian bodies. I then unpack how Shepherd's act of crying, coming from the position of a University TA, reveals Shepherd's own underprivileged (yet still privileged) positionality.

Privilege, positionality, unpack... it was all so predictable. Though, admittedly, I hadn't heard "minoritarian bodies" before.

The PhD student wrote that I was a "crypto-conservative" white supremacist, and a bad teacher. His blog post was (of course) published on a site called "Hot Mess Nasty Feminism."

Thankfully, writer Uri Harris pushed back against this line of thought in Quillette, arguing:[56]

> It makes sense to consider power dynamics when considering Shepherd's Laurier meeting, as part of a broader analysis. Yet, it makes very little sense to do so based on a historical narrative of white women and men of colour. A far more useful analysis would consider the fact that Shepherd was outnumbered three to one, or that Rambukkana is her supervisor, or that a person from the office of Gendered Violence Protection and Support was in the meeting. These things explain the power dynamics in the meeting quite well, it seems to me, while race and gender explain almost nothing. The fact that some of Shepherd's critics want to invoke a historical narrative of 'white woman plays the victim-card to get man of colour in trouble' to explain the meeting suggests a deeper ideological commitment.

Many of the academics and pundits who were grasping at straws to read race into the Laurier incident suggested I deployed "white tears" to somehow manipulate everyone else. But anyone listening to the tape in good faith can see that I am not intentionally crying in the meeting. I wish I hadn't cried – it would have been nice to appear stronger and more resolute – but I simply have the tendency to cry when I am under pressure.

*

On December 18, 2017, a statement from Laurier President Deborah MacLatchy was unexpectedly released:

> *I believe it is time for some clarity around the events of the past few weeks here at Wilfrid Laurier University, stemming from the very regrettable meeting that followed the showing of a TVO clip by a teaching assistant (TA) during a tutorial.*

> *[...]*

> *When the issue first broke, I erred on the side of caution. As a person, and as the president of Laurier, I am sensitive to the viewpoints and concerns of our students, staff and faculty. As an employer, I am cognisant that the four people who were in that meeting room are employees and one is also a student. All four are entitled to due process. I did not want to rush to judgement; rather, I wanted to ensure we were able to objectively assess the facts and make sound decisions flowing from that assessment.*

> *We hired an external fact-finder with expertise in human resources issues. I have received the report and we are taking decisive action to ensure these events will not be repeated. The report, along with what we already knew, has led me to the following conclusions and actions.*

> *There were numerous errors in judgement made in the handling of the meeting with Ms. Lindsay Shepherd, the TA of the tutorial in question. In fact, the meeting never should have happened at all. **No formal complaint, nor informal concern relative to a Laurier policy, was registered***

about the screening of the video [emphasis added]. *This was confirmed in the fact-finding report.*

The errors in judgement were compounded by misapplication of existing university policies and procedures. Basic guidelines and best practices on how to appropriately execute the roles and responsibilities of staff and faculty were ignored or not understood.

Procedures in how to apply university policies and under what circumstances were not followed. The training of key individuals to meet the expectations of the university in addressing an issue such as this was not sufficient and must be improved.

There was also institutional failure that allowed this to happen. And when there is institutional failure, responsibility ultimately starts and ends with me.

[...]

Specifically:

There was no wrongdoing on the part of Ms. Shepherd in showing the clip from TVO in her tutorial. Showing a TVO clip for the purposes of an academic discussion is a reasonable classroom teaching tool. Any instructional material needs to be grounded in the appropriate academic underpinnings to put it in context for the relevance of the learning outcomes of the course. The ensuing discussion also needs to be handled properly. We have no reason to believe this discussion was not handled well in the tutorial in question.

I have apologized to Ms. Shepherd publicly, as has Dr. Rambukkana, her supervising professor. The university has conveyed to her today the results of the fact-finding report, to make sure she understands it is clear that she was involved in no wrongdoing. The university is taking concrete steps to make changes to ensure this doesn't happen again.

It has been made clear to those who were involved in the meeting with Ms. Shepherd that their conduct does not meet the high standards I set for staff and faculty.

As these are individual employment issues, I cannot go into greater detail on any individual case. But know that the university has, and is, taking action to rectify the situation and send a clear signal that this cannot and will not happen again.

One key improvement highlighted is the need to enhance our faculty and TA training. It is the responsibility of course instructors to develop guidelines for the roles and expectations of their TAs. The university also has high expectations of professors as TA supervisors. We recognize the need to do more in this area. The university's intent is to enhance the training and support for both TA supervisors and teaching assistants, making these mandatory and standardized, for clarity and consistency across the university.

GENDERED AND SEXUAL VIOLENCE POLICY

It has become clear to us that managing the new Gendered and Sexual Violence Policy (GSVP) has led to a confusion in its application. In fact, the interviews conducted by the fact-finder confirmed that the rationale for invoking the GSVP did not exist. It was misapplied and was a significant overreach.

To provide clarity of the policy's intent and to strengthen accountability, we will engage in an administrative review with the goal of finding the appropriate structure to oversee and execute the GSVP and its accompanying procedures. We will also undertake a full review of the policy and its procedures.

In the interim, we will ensure access to the existing support and complaints procedures by providing management and oversight through the Office of Dispute Resolution and Support. This has the added benefit of improved accountability as that office reports through to me as president.

ACADEMIC FREEDOM AND FREEDOM OF EXPRESSION

For those who have chosen to use this incident as an indictment of Wilfrid Laurier University or the plight of Canadian universities in general, I say your assertion is unreasonable and unfounded. Laurier has a clear commitment to academic freedom and freedom of expression.

Laurier prepares our students and instructors for difficult discussions. We support our teachers in navigating complex and divisive issues with care and confidence. We are leaders in ensuring our students, faculty and staff have the necessary supports and tools to help those who have experienced marginalization and discrimination to engage fully. Properly grounded academic debate at Laurier occurs every day and encourages critical thinking and civil discourse. Ideas that one finds objectionable should be challenged and debated. The common good of society depends upon the search for knowledge and its free expression.

Free expression and academic freedom at the university require accompanying responsibilities and accountabilities to be met by members of the university community. We will continue to ensure we are protecting against, and dealing with, hate and intolerance. Those have no place in civil society, let alone on a university campus. They will not be tolerated at Laurier. I remain concerned by the way faculty, staff and students involved in aspects of this situation were targeted with such vitriol. Members of the university community must be supported to work and study in an environment free of discrimination and harassment and they have my commitment we will continue to make this a university priority.

It bears repeating in the current context that Laurier's support for our lesbian, gay, bi, trans, queer and two-spirited (LGBTQ2S) campus community and transgender people in particular is unwavering. In light of recent events, we have created and communicated additional supports for LGBTQ2S students, faculty and staff, and added measures to improve campus safety.

We will ensure that all students, staff and faculty know exactly what our commitment to academic freedom and freedom of expression means in the classroom. To that end we have established the Task Force on Freedom of Expression to take input from our community, look at best practices beyond Laurier, and develop a clear, tangible set of practical, implementable guidelines that will bring clarity to this issue for our own classrooms, and will have the potential to serve as best practices for others. That is my commitment to you.

MOVING FORWARD

Laurier offers an incredible student experience and exemplifies excellence in teaching, research and scholarship. I know this. Our students, faculty and staff know this. Our alumni know this. Our supporters and community partners know this. Our application numbers are outpacing last year's high level, demonstrating that prospective students know this as well.

Today, we turn the page on a very unfortunate incident. We are here to make sure it does not happen again. We are here to put an end to the ongoing politicization of this issue. And we are here to seize the opportunity to lead in developing useful tools for the classroom to ensure challenging, academically grounded debate thrives at Laurier and that others can learn from what we develop.

Deborah MacLatchy, PhD

President and Vice-Chancellor, Wilfrid Laurier University

I'm sure Wilfrid Laurier University would love to just *turn the page*, and make everything disappear. They would prefer to act like this situation was a total fluke, unconnected to any wider societal issues or phenomena. And while the letter claims that Laurier conveyed the results of the fact-finding report to me, they in fact only emailed me a copy of this public press release. The full fact-finding report was confidential, and no one aside from MacLatchy and perhaps a couple others in her office would see it.

But here is the kicker – the most important takeaway from MacLatchy's carefully crafted memo: *"No formal complaint, nor informal concern relative to a Laurier policy, was registered about the screening of the video. This was confirmed in the fact-finding report."*

No formal or informal complaint was registered. In other words, Rambukkana, Pimlott, and Joel had invented the complaints. That's why they wouldn't, and couldn't, specify who complained, or how many people complained. Did Rambukkana, Pimlott, and Joel call the now-infamous meeting for the purpose of intimidating me into pushing their worldview?

The university issued a clarification a couple days later in regard to that phrase:

> *Following the Dec. 18 statement on the independent fact-finder report noting 'No formal complaint, nor informal concern relative to a Laurier policy, was registered about the screening of the video,' there have been accusations in the media that the professors lied about or fabricated concerns that led to the meeting with Lindsay Shepherd. The university would like to emphasize that this is not the case. While no complaint was filed by a student in the tutorial, a later discussion among students about the video was brought to the attention of a staff member, who then brought it forward as a concern to the two professors, which led to the meeting.*

"A later discussion among students…" Okay, were the students present in the tutorial, or was everyone playing a game of telephone, and talking about something they had heard from someone else? It was also entirely possible that some students were speaking positively about the tutorial, and a Diversity & Equity official overheard and contacted Rambukkana. The question of why Pimlott – a professor who had nothing to do with my TAship or the tutorial –got involved was never addressed.

Seeing as Wilfrid Laurier University was very eager to proclaim their all-encompassing commitment to free speech, I figured that next semester, I would test whether their words were empty or not.

PART II

CHAPTER 13

On my first day back on campus in January 2018, I flicked on the lights to the TA mailroom, and opened the cabinet with the TA mail cubbies. To my surprise, my mail slot was stacked with letters. I double-checked the envelopes: indeed, they were all addressed to me, sent from various locations in the US and Canada. There was even one from France.

"I applaud you!" read one letter from a former academic in the US. "Most importantly, for standing up for free speech against your inquisitors; and secondarily, for recording the 'interview.'"

Another read simply, "Lindsay: Hero."

One man sent a picture of me cut out from the newspaper – I recognized it from the day of the free speech rally.

"Don't be angry with me, because I am sending you the photo that National Post published! I have sound reasons, if there ever was or is a photo worth 1000 words – this is the one – a stern, determined but yet gentle woman!"

One woman wrote, "I couldn't even gag my way through that apology/explanation letter from the large bearded fellow – give me a break!"

I kept every single letter. But because I had no reason to trust anyone at the university, I always thought at the back of my mind that maybe I had more mail, but the TAs or faculty with access to the communal mailroom had stolen some letters or packages. I had no evidence of such a thing. But, it would be easy enough for them, there were no cameras in the office. I would never know, but I always wondered.

I walked through the halls of the Dr. Alvin Woods Building, where the arts department offices lined the hallways. The office doors of

Rambukkana and Pimlott were stripped bare of the posters that were previously displayed. Neither of them were teaching any classes this semester or the next: if you searched their names in the course offerings database, nothing showed up. Adria Joel's name had been quietly removed from the Diversity & Equity Office staff list. Likewise, Herbert Pimlott's name had been removed from the graduate program coordinator contact section on the MA CAST website, and replaced by another professor's. All of their social media accounts were still locked down or deleted. Rambukkana, Pimlott, and Joel were just… gone. And the university wasn't saying anything about where they were or when they were coming back.

With the start of the new year, I was fueled by a desire to bring back a culture of free discussion and free expression to the Wilfrid Laurier University campus. I joined together with three student acquaintances that had reached out to me during the controversy and we created a club called the Laurier Society for Open Inquiry (LSOI). LSOI's three-point mandate was to (1) Promote intellectual curiosity, open inquiry, and freedom of expression; (2) Provide alternatives to the dominant societal narrative; and (3) Build a community of thinkers who enjoy partaking in reasonable, nuanced discussion.

We quickly surpassed one hundred official members – we permitted anyone to join. Three Laurier faculty became key members and supporters of the club: business professor William McNally, religion and culture professor David Haskell, and sport humanities professor Jordan Goldstein.

LSOI's first event of 2018 was symbolic: we screened the entire "Genders, Rights, and Freedom of Speech" episode of The Agenda – the infamous episode I had shown five minutes of in my CS101 class. A school newspaper writer from The Cord covered the event, and though the author made a few digs at us, I actually found the review portion of the article, "Attending a meeting at Laurier Society for Open Inquiry,"[57] quite flattering:

Have you heard of the Laurier Society for Open Inquiry (LSOI)? It's a club that Lindsay Shepherd recently started with a handful of undergraduate students. On her twitter account, she describes it as "a club to promote the open exchange of ideas".

As more information about the Shepherd controversy was released, I found myself increasingly in the camp that disapproved of Shepherd's actions and the way they were portrayed in the media. I didn't have high expectations for LSOI, but for the sake of being fair, I decided to attend their first meeting and tried to be open before drawing conclusions.

On the evening of Jan. 31, I trekked across campus to the science building.

Shepherd and some of the club executives stood by the door. They smiled at me as I went in.

Inside, the large hall was a little over half full.

The audience was mostly composed of male students. Some Laurier faculty members and non-Laurier students were in attendance as well. Many of them were dressed nicely and there was a sense of excitement in the air.

After Shepherd and the executives introduced themselves and the club, they moved to the projector to set up.

The audience settled in for the focus of the meeting — a full screening of the The Agenda's episode on Bill C-16.

"Hey Anton [one of the club executives]", Shepherd interjected coyly, "is heckling allowed?"

To heckle means to interrupt the presentation with jeering, cheering or applause. According to the executives, heckling was not only allowed, but encouraged. This caused a wave of laughter to ripple over the audience.

Despite that however, most of the episode was watched in a respectful silence.

When it finished the executives turned on the lights. Anton peeked through the door and jokingly congratulated the other executives for "playing a full Jordan Peterson clip without SJWs bursting into the lecture halls".

The executives then opened the floor for discussion, which to me consisted of familiar sentiments about how "the radical left can't handle rational debate," and how "neo-Marxist ideology is overtaking campus." At about the 30-minute mark, I left.

LSOI also held pub nights that featured guest talks like "Free Speech on Campus: A Lawyer's Perspective" by lawyer James Kitchen from the Justice Centre for Constitutional Freedoms, and "Ideological Conformity in Politics and the Media" by Andrew Lawton, a conservative commentator. This was the good life: a gathering of open-minded people who wanted to discuss ideas over some food and drinks at a tavern in uptown Waterloo.

I had loved speaker's forums and public lectures since I was a first-year student, and was happy I now had the resources and audience base to create my own events. Public lectures were a great way to gain knowledge and get a sampling of the work being done out in the world without enrolling in an entire class about the topic. And because these public events were also often free to attendees, they were accessible to everyone.

To some detractors, running a free expression-related club out of passion and interest was beyond the realm of believability. Some people claimed I was only running the club to push a right-wing agenda. Funnily enough, I travelled to a country club-type place in Toronto to meet with two individuals who were interested in giving LSOI $10,000 of Koch Brothers money. But I must not have had enough of a right-wing agenda, because after meeting with me and hearing about LSOI's commitment to hearing different perspectives, they decided not to give us the money.

Others claimed I was running LSOI just to stay relevant. It was an accusation I saw with some frequency on social media, that everything I was doing was for attention. I couldn't do anything or say anything without being accused of wanting attention. "I feel you've crossed the boundary from someone who went to the public for help against ideological repression, to someone who courts that attention," one man wrote to me. A Laurier student messaged me on Twitter saying, "It's unfortunate that so many other wonderful TAs need to be out shined [sic] by your need for attention."

Yet, if for a period of time I was laying low and not active on social media, people would immediately proclaim that I was now irrelevant, no one cared about me anymore, and my fifteen minutes was up. People have been announcing to me that my fifteen minutes is up for the last couple years. I didn't see why that was such a popular go-to insult for people. In my mind, there was nothing wrong with temporarily being in the spotlight to make an impact and highlight issues of public importance, and then resuming what you were previously doing in your life. There was value in those cultural moments – they punctuated our history.

Similarly, people loved proclaiming that they used to like me, but because of a certain opinion I recently expressed, they are going to unfollow me on Twitter and they are no longer a supporter. It was as if they enjoyed putting me on a pedestal, because they then held the power to throw me off of it.

I heard it all. I was just an attention whore, I wanted my fifteen minutes, I was using my appearance to get support from gullible men. I was too young and impressionable; I was a naive little girl letting myself be radicalized by the alt-right. I was so intellectually unprincipled and empty-headed that I ran over to the right after the left was mean to me. I was being used; powerful men were using me to advance their own agendas. Conservatives and right-wingers were using me to promote their own ideologies. I was a 20-something with no understanding of the world, and I would regret everything I've done later down the road.

I figured that if I was a late middle-aged woman, I wouldn't be subject to the bulk of these accusations. In some ways, I looked forward to ageing.

*

In the first week of January, the other TAs and I had a meeting with our new professor-supervisor for Communication Studies 101, Judith Nicholson. Nicholson's area of academic expertise was "black mobilities."

Nicholson had sent us our CS101 course syllabus in late December, and I noticed the electronic document had a statement, right under the course title at the top of the page, that read "We acknowledge that we live, learn and work on the traditional territories of the Neutral, Anishnawbe and Haudenosaunee peoples." I found land acknowledgments to be a way for guilt-ridden people to absolve themselves of the burden they felt due to the sins of their colonialist ancestors. They would utter that they are living on stolen land, or on land that "traditionally'" belongs to an indigenous group; even though they had no intention of ever giving the land back or removing themselves from the land. I figured that if you want to give land acknowledgments, fine – but then you must also be actively working to physically give the land back to indigenous peoples.

On Twitter, I posted a screenshot of the land acknowledgment and commented, "I wonder how indigenous people feel about the holier-than-thou 'SJWs' who use land acknowledgments to virtue signal. This land acknowledgment is on a course syllabus. I see them in email signatures too."

At that first group meeting with Judith Nicholson and the other TAs, Nicholson said in her introductory remarks that as TAs of her course, we were prohibited from slandering or defaming the university, through social media or otherwise.

She turned to me.

"Lindsay, I don't do the whole Twitter thing, but I heard you posted my syllabus on your Twitter."

"Oh, I only posted something about the little land acknowledgment at the top, I didn't post the actual course content of your syllabus," I answered.

"Yeah, I'm going to need you to delete that tweet. That is a violation of my intellectual property."

"Sorry, Dr. Nicholson," I replied carefully, "But I'm not quite sure what you mean by that being your intellectual property. I don't think I am actually required to delete that tweet."

"So, you will have to delete the tweet," she snapped, "And if you don't, I will be notifying the deans that you have breached copyright law and Laurier's non-academic code of conduct, and that could result in you getting a note on your file."

Judith said all this, of course, not in a private one-on-one with me, but in front of the other five TAs, as a sort of performance. Judith exchanged a brief smug glance with the other TAs, who were lapping it up.

"Okay, well, unfortunately, I do not see the grounds for deleting the tweet, so I do not really see myself doing that," I said in a polite tone.

"Well," Nicholson sighed, "I'll be contacting the deans, then. Moving on."

What a great first day with my new supervisor!

If I had been complimenting the land acknowledgment, Judith Nicholson would have no problem with my tweet. But because I was critiquing it, I was being threatened on the bogus grounds of intellectual property law and misconduct. That land acknowledgment was an institution-wide statement; it was in no way Nicholson's original intellectual work.

I reported the tale of Judith Nicholson's threats on my Twitter account. Very quickly after, I got an email from Dean of Arts Richard Nemesvari:

> *Dear Ms. Shepherd,*
>
> *It has come to my attention that you were told that the Laurier land acknowledgement statement for the CS101 syllabus is the intellectual property of the faculty member creating the syllabus, and that copying or communicating that part of the syllabus is a breach of intellectual property. That is incorrect. There is no breach of copyright in posting the university land acknowledgement statement. There is likewise no breach of the university Non-academic Code of Conduct.*
>
> *All the best.*

The Communication Studies faculty just couldn't help themselves. They kept making up their own rules as they went along. I was just lucky that I had a way, through my Twitter account, to call them out.

CHAPTER 14

The courses I was taking in the Winter 2018 semester were my electives, so I could fortunately escape much of the overdone postmodernism and poststructuralism from last semester and experience some variety. I was taking a Cultural Analysis and Social Theory course called Past Violence and Public Action, which was about the politics and practices of memorialization. I was also in a Communication Studies course called Risk, Media, and Science, and one English class – Cosmetics, Aesthetics, and the Beautiful. One of the activities we had to do in the English course was bring in two cosmetic products from home, and as a class sort the products into categories such as shape, colour, or purpose, and write a paper on our experience categorizing the products. Canadian liberal arts graduate degrees had lost almost all prestige to me at this point.

I had quite an impressive number of speaking engagements lined up in the winter semester: four in the month of February and one in March. But my first panel discussion as a featured speaker was to be at Saint Mary's University in Halifax on January 25, 2018 – I was invited by Dr. Mark Mercer, President of the Society for Academic Freedom and Scholarship.

In addition to relaying the story of the Laurier affair at these speaking engagements, I would also speak about the importance of free expression, where the tendency to censor originates from, and the state of free speech on campus more generally. Because my MA research paper was on the topic of free speech on campus, I could write my paper and prepare my speaking notes in tandem.

A few days before my flight to Nova Scotia, I trekked up to the MA CAST student lounge on campus to print off some readings to keep me occupied during the flight. I tapped my student card on the door reader and entered the lounge, but the printer wasn't working.

I left the room and went one floor down, to try the printer in the Communication Studies lounge. I tapped my student card, entered when the little light went green, and sat down at one of the computer stations. The printer worked. I stacked and stapled my readings as the machine spat the pages out. I heard the door behind me click open – I turned to see Ethan, the trans activist MA Communication Studies student who said "violence is okay" during his speech at the Trans Solidarity Rally, and who had been tweeting at me for the past couple months. I turned back to my computer station, but I saw from the corner of my eye that Ethan hadn't moved from the doorway – he was still standing there, staring at me. I ignored him.

"Um, what are you doing here?" he finally said.

"Printing," I replied, gesturing to the humming printer.

"You are not supposed to be in here, this is a space for communication students."

I rolled my eyes to myself. I was a Communication Studies TA taking a Communication Studies graduate class whose student card allowed me access to the room.

"I'm just using the printer. The one upstairs isn't working."

"This is a space for Communication students only," he repeated. "You should not be in here."

"Are you going to tweet about it?" I deadpanned.

"You have to leave now," he said. "You cannot be in here."

"You are petty and pathetic," I muttered, still facing my screen.

"What?" he shrieked.

I turned around and faced him.

"I said, you are petty and pathetic."

He scoffed dramatically and stormed out of the lounge.

A couple of weeks later, when I was passing by that same room, out of curiosity I tested my student card to see if my room permissions were still intact after that interaction with Ethan. He was definitely the type who would go tell the higher-ups to take away my access because I was making it an unsafe space. I tapped my card on the electronic reader at the door. My suspicions were correct. It flashed red this time, and there was no familiar click of the door unlocking. My ability to enter the room had been inexplicably revoked. I tested my card on the upstairs lounge and a couple of the other office spaces – it flashed green as usual. It was only the Communication Studies lounge that I was now barred from entering.

*

A couple hours before my first speaking event at Saint Mary's University, I did a smaller, complementary Q&A session at a neighbouring institution, Mount Saint Vincent University, organized by professor Steve Perrott.

As we approached the door to the small auditorium, I noticed a sign that said the room assignment had changed – the sign directed the Q&A attendees to another room number. "Oh, are we in a different room?" I asked Dr. Perrott. "No," he said, puzzled, examining the sign. "This is all the way across campus…"

Detractors were trying to confuse potential audience members and give them directions elsewhere, in order to prevent them from attending the event. I would learn that it is quite a common tactic. I also found out that the Mount Saint Vincent University Students' Union (MSVUSU) had posted a statement on their official Facebook page that said:

> The MSVUSU is committed to fighting against transphobia and white supremacy.
>
> As some of you may be aware, Lindsay Shepherd has been invited by a professor and will be on campus at 12 pm to do a Q&A with students and faculty. Shepherd gained attention after facing repercussions at Wilfred [sic] Laurier University for showing a transphobic video of Jordan Peterson in a tutorial and has since gone public in defence of her decision. Since then Shepherd has gained significant support from alt-right groups and white supremacists, who champion her under the banner of free speech. We want to be clear that we understand that hate speech is not free speech. Trans peoples [sic] existence is not an opinion to be debated, and we are committed to supporting our trans, racialized and indigenous students on campus.
>
> We will be opening up the Wellness Centre from 12-1:30 to provide a decompression space and welcome all those who need a place on campus at that time.

It was surprising to me that my presence on a university campus meant that the Wellness Centre needed to open a "decompression space" for the duration of my visit.

The Q&A session went well, though a trans activist in attendance accused me of hate speech, to which I countered, (quite gently, mind you), "Are you familiar with sections 318 and 319 of the Criminal Code, which define hate speech as promoting genocide or inciting hatred?"

If I had really committed hate speech by showing a TVO clip, then I presumably would have already received some sort of legal notice. The trans activist, flustered, answered that they had a learning disability and couldn't remember laws, and then fled the room with a cry of "Fuck transphobia" or something of the sort.

The event at Saint Mary's University was much more dramatic. A contingent of Marxists, led by a man in combat boots, arrived at the event and began handing out flyers to attendees titled "Why are Neo-Nazis Concerned with Freedom of Speech? Lindsay Shepherd and the Far-Right," which contained a screed about how free speech was for "Trumpite bigots." The Marxists handed out "Alt-Right Bingo" cards and sat down with bingo daubers. The bingo sheet had terms like "Authoritarian Leftist," "Viewpoint Diversity," "Open Exchange of Ideas," and "Virtue Signal." Whenever a speaker on the panel used one of the terms, the Marxists would all dab their sheets, making an audible fuss about it. None of them got a bingo. It was kind of a funny and clever thing to do – it was true that some of the terms were certainly a daily part of the free speech crowd's vocabulary – but there was no way the terms they included were alt-right. That was a real stretch. Once the Q&A portion opened up, the other panelists and I were incessantly accused of white supremacy, Nazism, neo-Nazism, hate speech, and bigotry by the Marxists dominating the mic.

At one point, I said over the mic, in response to one of the Marxists, that I was not a Nazi. It felt borderline degrading to have to even respond to such a far-fetched, crazy accusation.

Despite the stress of the relentless accusations that I was somehow complicit in Nazism, I had a fun and lively dinner with some faculty and student attendees from the event. Professor Perrott said to me before he departed for the evening, "You may not be on the right side of history, but you're on the right side of justice."

The next morning, I had lemon ricotta pancakes at the hotel restaurant and spent the day roaming around the Canadian Museum of Immigration at Pier 21 before heading to the airport and flying back to Ontario.

*

At the end of January, I set out to Toronto with a few Laurier Society for Open Inquiry pals to see Jordan Peterson speak at the University of Toronto's Wycliffe College on a panel titled "The Meaning of Life: Three Perspectives."

I had grown to very much admire Jordan Peterson. Back in the Laurier interrogation, I said I didn't agree with Jordan Peterson – but perhaps it was more that I was just unsure about the whole Bill C-16 matter, and unconfident about siding with someone who seemed to be so hated by my professors. I was now often searching clips of Jordan Peterson on YouTube, listening to them as I washed dishes, folded laundry, and swept my floors. Cleaning was a very pleasant activity when you had something interesting to listen to. It was strange to see so many academics and pundits sneering at Peterson and proclaiming he was a bad person – a misogynist, a transphobe, a charlatan, what have you – when it struck me, from his facial expressions, mannerisms, and way of speaking, that he was a truly good person.

That evening in Toronto, I met Dr. Peterson for the first time. From afar, I saw him sitting at a desk signing books, but there were at least 50 people in the line, clutching their copies of *12 Rules for Life*. I was even stopped by a few people who wanted me to autograph their books.

I was hanging out in a hallway, about to leave, when I saw Peterson walking towards me in the halls, escorted by security for a washroom break. I smiled at him. He almost walked right past me, but luckily he noticed me, backed up, and shook my hand. We exchanged a quick greeting – he had to get back to his long lineup of fans. It is still the only time I have met him in person to this day.

Despite my growing admiration for Peterson, I felt the thing I could do for him that would most convey my respect was to leave him alone. I thought about the overwhelming amount of emails and interview requests I was receiving, and knew he was probably getting 500 times more: the best thing I could do was admire him from afar and avoid burdening him with being yet another person to exchange emails with. I was also conscious that my name was very much wrapped up with Peterson's, and I was not interested in glomming onto his fame.

*

Over the month of February, I spoke at Harvard University for the Open Campus Initiative, the Confederation Club in Kitchener, UBC Okanagan, and Franklin & Marshall College in Lancaster, Pennsylvania. Lancaster was perhaps my favourite location: I got to stay in a stately colonial guesthouse. I walked down to a local brewery both evenings I was there, where I sat at the bar alone with a pint of red ale, thinking about how much I loved travelling to America, and seeing its geographical diversity and fascinating regional cultures. The host professor who invited me to Lancaster took me to the Barnes Foundation in Philadelphia the day after my speech, where I became an admirer of the art of Renoir and Modigliani.

It was only after I had written a couple guest op-eds and accepted a few speaking invitations that Prof. Haskell, who was well-versed in the media world, said to me, "You're getting paid for all this, right?"

"…No?" I answered.

He laughed. "Well, you should be."

I had erroneously assumed that op-eds and speaking events functioned the same way as TV or radio interviews: you accept the invitations for the exposure and chance to spread your message, and no money was on the table. But often when you receive an invitation to speak or write a guest op-ed, there is no mention or offer of money either because the inviter doesn't want to make assumptions about the monetary worth of your services, or because they're hoping they can get your labour for free. It is up to you, the invitee, to tactfully ask about an honorarium.

I also received a special email in February, from the Laurier Centre for Teaching Innovation and Excellence, notifying me that I had been nominated for the 2018 Laurier Student Teaching Award of Excellence.

"The initial selection committee met recently and was truly impressed by the positive contributions you have made to the student learning experience at Laurier," the email read. I smirked.

"The committee reviewed over 170 submissions during this initial selection period, making the decision process extremely difficult. Unfortunately, you were not selected to submit a nomination package for review by the adjudication committee."

Darn, what a shame!

"Although you were not selected as a finalist in the award process, your contribution to teaching and learning at Laurier is inspiring and positively impacts our community. We will be holding an event in the Fall to celebrate all winners, finalists, and nominees for this award. Please stay tuned for an invitation!"

Lovely! However, months later, I came across photos of the 2018 teaching awards gala posted on social media. How curious... I hadn't ever received my promised invitation.

CHAPTER 15

Just after Christmastime back in 2017, free speech advocate professors William McNally and David Haskell had gone on Jordan Peterson's YouTube channel to talk about the Laurier controversy. After they finished recording, Peterson indicated to McNally that he would come speak at Laurier if we organized an event to host him. But in the winter and spring of 2018, Peterson was on an international book tour, and so I don't hold it against him that no LSOI event with him ever transpired, though it would have been legendary.

The club members and I still wanted to have a big-ticket speaking event, and thought about who we could invite that would make a splash and get our club some attention. We needed the speaker to be an Ontarian, as we didn't have the funds to fly anyone in. One of the club executives, Anton, suggested Faith Goldy. I didn't know much about her, but Anton said he would handle the invitation and communication process. Easy enough, I figured – takes some of the workload off of me – so I gave him the green-light. I knew Goldy advocated for lower immigration levels and was fired from her position as a commentator with Rebel Media for appearing on an alt-right podcast, but as someone who had been completely unaware of the intensity of the culture wars in 2016 and early 2017, I didn't know how easily any mention of her pushed peoples' buttons. Originally, LSOI was organizing an open borders versus closed borders debate, with Goldy taking the "closed borders" side, but no one would agree to take on the "open borders" position and debate her. We decided we would still have her come in to speak, but because it couldn't be a debate, we would launch the "Unpopular Opinions Speaker Series," with this being its first event.

Goldy's presentation was set to be March 20, 2018 – Professor McNally booked the room. We put up posters around campus advertising the event, but the posters would often be ripped down within hours. Some of the culprits were all too happy to identify themselves –

one Communication Studies instructor boasted on Twitter about tearing down the posters.[58]

An opposing poster campaign was launched to counter the LSOI event. One night on campus, I witnessed two hooded individuals dressed in all black taping posters around campus that read "#NoNazisAtLaurier." A protest to our event had been declared.

The undergraduate and graduate students' unions released a joint statement, "Re: Unpopular Speaker Series," that read "Our campus community benefits from rigorous academic debate. Not all debate, however, meets this standard. Sometimes 'unpopular' opinions are simply ignorant and complicit in the spread of hate and bigotry."

The statement denounced the LSOI event as a "weaponization of free speech [that] ultimately supresses [sic] open debate and prevents many in our community from feeling recognized, valued, and included."[59]

On March 19, Judith Nicholson sent an email to all of her TAs cancelling our weekly meeting on March 20, writing "A student group has invited white supremacist and neo-Nazi supporter Faith Goldy to speak on campus tomorrow evening. With demonstrations being planned, I want to ensure that you will have the option to stay off campus if you wish."

That same day, LSOI was mentioned in GQ magazine, in a March 19, 2018 article called "The Free Speech Grifters."[60] It certainly wasn't a piece meant to commend the club: it claimed we were amongst the free speech clubs whose only purpose was to "trigger the libs." While I might cede that point for the Goldy event – that being intentionally provocative was a motivating factor for us – I considered LSOI a serious club that I thought really fostered a sense of community. I figured that ultimately, it's not very damning if the worst thing someone can accuse you of is being a little provocative. In fact, I considered it a positive quality. I liked people with an edge. Many pundits and thinkers openly disdained provocateurs, calling them unprincipled, but I maintained that provocation could be done in earnest.

Most of the LSOI events I had held thus far were small, low-key pub nights, where people from all walks of life gathered at communal dining tables and chatted with their neighbours. But because a protest was declared against the Faith Goldy event, media interest and attention went through the roof, as it always does when a protest is announced.

*

On March 20, 2018, protesters were gathering outside the university on the grass quad under a purple glow from the sunset. I wanted to check out the protest for a few minutes before going inside to manage my own event. A lineup of hundreds of people trying to get into the auditorium to see Goldy speak had already formed.

Hanging from the nearby residence building was a big white sheet with ominous black paint that read "Laurier enables white supremacy." Protesters were drumming and screaming "No Nazis at Laurier." Rainbow Centre affiliates were handing out signs that read "Laurier Facilitates White Supremacy" and "Not On My Campus." Others had brought their own signs, with messages like "Your definition of free speech = Hate Speech."[61]

As I was walking through the protest, I spotted a couple of my classmates and professors all standing together. Professor Greg Bird, who had tweeted earlier in the day, "Is @Laurier a university or a Nazi recruitment centre?"[62] was amongst them.

The MC at the demonstration was a local artist who called herself a "hard femme queer radical." I tuned into the protest chants for a bit. "Hey hey! Ho ho! White supremacy's got to go!" A speaker took the stage and talked about the cultural appropriation of adding yogurt to hummus. Toby from the Rainbow Centre went up to explain that a "buddy system" was in effect for the protest, and that everyone in the audience should find a buddy to keep them safe and accompany them to the washroom.

But alas, I couldn't listen to the rest of the protest's speaker lineup, as I had to make my way to my own event.

While I was manning the membership form table for people buying LSOI memberships, two girls handed me pieces of paper that read "Fuck Nazis." (I kept those scraps of paper for my memorabilia box). At one point in the night, a man tried to forcefully push a makeshift Ku Klux Klan robe he had brought into my hands. It was all so performative; as if these activists enjoyed the live-action roleplay of a Nazi Germany or Jim Crow South simulation. I genuinely got the sense that they derived pleasure from pretending they lived in a world where they were the heroes fighting against forces of evil. But in reality, this was just one night of a speech about Canadian immigration policy on a university campus, where the speaker would be tested and questioned on her opinions after she had finished her PowerPoint.

Finally, we hustled 150 attendees into the room, reaching capacity, and the rest of the line was turned away.

Professor McNally kicked off the housekeeping remarks. He only got through a few seconds of his notes before the blare of a fire alarm rang through my ears. And just like that, within a minute, the event was over.

"May I just say, that's a very irresponsible, juvenile thing to do!" Professor McNally yelled over the alarm as the audience filed out disappointedly.

"It's against the human rights code to give space to someone who is actively oppressing people with their words and beliefs," Janice Jo Lee, the protest leader, said that night on a TV news broadcast about the event's cancellation.[63]

Everything these people didn't like was against the human rights code.

The Record reported on the event's derailment, and got a quote from Ethan Jackson about it:[64]

> *Ethan Jackson, a 26-year-old graduate student at Laurier who helped organize the demonstration, said he was happy with the way the evening turned out.*
>
> *"Personally speaking, for my own self and not as an organizer, I am glad somebody was able to pull the alarm," he said, adding that he does not know who did it and that the organizers behind the demonstration did not suggest it happen.*
>
> *"Giving somebody who is a known white supremacist that kind of platform, is in no way academic freedom, it is in no way freedom of expression," he said.*

Laurier never did reveal who pulled the fire alarm. Very mysteriously, no camera footage was available in that particular hallway. Laurier refused to answer any questions about the fire alarm, and over time, people stopped asking about it. In similar cases in the US and Canada, when masked, hooded figures pulled fire alarms, the perpetrator was identified swiftly, in a police investigation. But not at Laurier.

Out of principle, LSOI attempted to re-book Goldy for an event on April 30, 2018, alongside University of New Brunswick professor Dr. Ricardo Duchesne. We wanted to make a point of fighting back against her de-platforming while adding an academic element by inviting Professor Duchesne. When Laurier proved unresponsive to our room booking requests, we sought out space at the University of Waterloo. They told me they were going to charge LSOI $1,400 for the theatre rental and another $1,400 for security. It was doable.

But when I met with the UWaterloo room booking coordinators and the university's head of security in person for a tour, I was given a new figure of $28,500. The justification for the inflated cost was the Toronto incel van attack of April 23 – their line of reasoning was that another incel van attack could very well happen at UWaterloo. We were priced out from holding the event, and it was cancelled.

I don't regret my decision to invite Goldy to speak at Laurier. All it was, at the end of the day, was a talk – a speaker invited to give a presentation to some members of a club, which everyone else had the option of ignoring. But one thing changed for me after the kerfuffle. A lot of free speech supporters had been desperate for a free speech advocate to come along who wouldn't associate in any way with the immigration debate, and I could no longer be that person for them. I would never be able to be the clean, uncompromised free speech advocate that those people were looking for, as I was fatally attracted to that which is taboo.

*

A few weeks later, LSOI hosted David Clement, an ardent libertarian and a director of Students for Liberty, to give a speech called "Why Canada Needs More Immigrants: Debunking the Alt-Right." We held the event at the Kitchener Public Library, as Laurier refused us event space. It was a great presentation, with a crowd of about 50. But, because there was no protest, the event went almost completely unnoticed.[65] Funny how when I hosted Goldy, I was bombarded with accusations that I was enabling the alt-right and I was too sympathetic to their opinions. But when I hosted an open borders libertarian, no one accused me of pushing his agenda, or being too sympathetic to his opinions.

Though the fuss over the Goldy event gradually died down, I'd be remiss not to mention an email I received in March 2018. One of my graduate course professors, Marta Marín-Dòmine, sent an email that read:

Latest developments have made me realize that it would be better to have the presentations in class done one by one. You will be entitled to invite a couple of your colleagues for the sake of debate and to share your newly acquired kowledge [sic].

Because our last month of classes was to consist only of graduate student presentations, this meant the remainder of our class was nominally cancelled. But the class would still be going on behind closed doors: professor Marín-Dòmine changed the program structure so that students could invite whoever they wanted to attend their own class presentations, which effectively meant that every other student in the class attended everyone else's presentations, with me being disinvited from all of them. On the first day of presentations, which started following one hour of the professor's lecture, Marín-Dòmine announced, "That's it for me, now it is time for student presentations. So, if you were invited to the student presentations for today, you can remain in the class, otherwise, feel free to spend this time how you see fit. You can use it to work on your research papers."

I got up to leave the classroom, as I hadn't been invited to any student presentations. But no one else budged; every other person remained in their seat. The new policy was really just a way to get me out of the room, so I couldn't watch or comment on any of the other presentations. It was a shame: I felt that observing the presentations of my colleagues was important for my own graduate school experience. Oh well.

Later in the month, a couple of Laurier students tagged me on Twitter to alert me that black stickers had been plastered on telephone poles and bus shelters across the street from the campus. The stickers said in white font, "Fucking Expel Lindsay Shepherd Already!" The word "Expel" had originally been spelled "Expell" – the second L had been scribbled out with black marker. When I was on the campus later that day, I did a stroll of the campus and found at least ten of the stickers myself, plastered on crosswalk stations and bus poles. I never tore them down. I thought they were funny, and it was kind of flattering that someone had spent the time and money to print these. And besides, expel me for what?

CHAPTER 16

The winter semester was coming to a close. I had to reschedule my last day of CS101 tutorials because of a speaking engagement I had at UC Berkeley – with the timing of flights, I wouldn't be able to get back in time to teach the class.

The protocol for rescheduling classes, Judith Nicholson had told us, was to either find a substitute TA; cancel class but include the content of the missed week in the next week's class; or reschedule with a mutually agreeable time with students.

I wanted to see my students one last time before the semester ended, so I sent them a Doodle poll and asked them to fill out which time blocks they could attend for a rescheduled tutorial. That week, once we settled on the three rescheduled tutorial blocks I would host, I sent an email to Judith Nicholson asking for her final approval of the plan.

> *Greetings Dr. Nicholson,*
>
> *Due to recent events, it will be impossible for me to be on campus on Friday the 23rd.*
>
> *However, I have polled the class on Doodle as to whether they would be open to rescheduling, and I am wondering if I may have your permission to implement this solution:*
>
> *Based on student availability, I split them into three grouped tutorials that I will host.*
>
> *Session 1: Monday March 26, 10:30-11:20am*
> *Session 2: Monday March 26, 1:30-2:20pm*
> *Session 3: Thursday March 29, 11:30am-12:20pm*

If you approve this, are you able to book classrooms for these sessions?

Thank you kindly,

Lindsay Shepherd

Nicholson replied the next day, and I noticed the names of the deans were copied in her reply. "I will not approve your plans," she wrote. "I will not book rooms for tutorials on Monday... I will instead send an email now to the other TAs instructing them to allow your students to join their tutorials next Wednesday and Thursday," she wrote. I howled with laughter as I read the next passage of her email: "I have copied Dean Nemesvari and Dean Deutschman on my reply because it is clear that you contacted students to re-schedule your tutorials before discussing with me. This is inappropriate, and so I want it to be noted."

This woman was still trying. Her original plan to get me in trouble over posting her indigenous land acknowledgment on Twitter had failed, so she was still grasping at straws, doing whatever she could to thwart my academic career.

I responded, "I fail to see the inappropriateness...you've mentioned that if a TA needs to miss a tutorial, there are three possible solutions: find a substitute; roll the missed week's content into the next week; or reschedule with a mutually agreeable time with students."

She wrote back: "Lindsay, This will be my last response to you on this matter... Yes, I outlined the solutions [above], and I noted they had to be done with my approval."

I replied, "Hi Dr. Nicholson, And I did indeed ask for your approval. Regards, Lindsay Shepherd."

But, as she had indicated, she stopped replying. She really thought I should have a note on my file from the deans for not asking her approval

176

to reschedule my tutorials, when the whole reason for my original email was to ask for her approval.

The deans she had copied in her emails were uninterested in her attempt to seek vengeance, and I never heard from them on the matter. I also never again corresponded with the dreadful Judith Nicholson.

*

In April 2018, our Major Research Paper proposal presentations came around: every student in the MA program was required to deliver a short summary of the research they were pursuing to get feedback from the department's professors, of which there were a handful in the room. When it was my turn, I pulled up my PowerPoint slides and talked about how I was going to delve into the subject of free speech. One of my slides, outlining the topics I was going to cover in my paper, read:

Free speech on campus as it relates to:

- *Historical context -- e.g. UC Berkeley Free Speech Movement 1960s*
- *The far-right*
- *Classical liberalism, libertarianism, individualism*
- *Gender and race*
- *Self-censorship*
- *Legalities -- hate propaganda laws*
- *Karl Popper's paradox of tolerance (1945)*
- *No-platforming*
- *Safe space culture*
- *Institutional statements on freedom of expression (U Chicago; UBC; WLU)*

I discussed some of the works I would be citing, such as Jonathan Rauch's "Kindly Inquisitors," Keith E. Whittington's "Speak Freely: Why

Universities Must Defend Free Speech," and John Stuart Mill's "On Liberty."

"Thank you! Any questions or comments?" I asked at the end of my 10-minute presentation.

Before I had finished my sentence, the hands of two professors shot up.

The first commenter was a male professor who muttered that universities must not platform hate speech, and that in his opinion, Faith Goldy was a "neo-Nazi bimbo" or "neo-Nazi Barbie." It was hard to hear exactly what he said through his mumbling. I had not mentioned Faith Goldy in my presentation, and neither had anyone else: he was making a dig at the LSOI event of last month. While every other student had received helpful comments and advice from their supervisors and the other professors, I was instead being pestered with a mumbling professor's thoughts about Faith Goldy.

"Okay," I said slowly, "Thank you for that, but how does that help me with my paper?" The seminar head, Professor Ironstone, murmured something indistinguishable, which prompted the professor to finally ask some sort of question from me.

"So, if you are committed to hearing different viewpoints, you must think university geography departments should teach flat earth theory, then?" he asked me.

I pursed my lips. Why did the enemies of free speech always bring up flat earth theory? Why did they think that was the comment that won them the argument against open inquiry and free thought? I responded that I was far more concerned with topics that had social currency, as demonstrated by media coverage, government attention, and popular interest.

The other professor who had her hand up, Jasmin Zine (a specialist in "Islamophobia Studies") then jumped in and ranted about how free speech leads to violence and hate. Zine had penned an op-ed about free speech back in December 2017, where she wrote:

> *Right-wing ideologues use free speech as an alibi for their transphobic and Islamophobic rhetoric. It has become a tool for related neo-fascist groups to mount campaigns of vandalism, harassment and intimidation. On my campus, colleagues have received death threats and transgender students have been harassed.*[66]

I shook my head after first coming across this article. Yet another professor claiming transgender students were being harassed on the Laurier campus while presenting no evidence. And remember: the "harassment" consisted of the Rainbow Centre receiving a dozen one-star Facebook reviews and a few emails criticizing their programming.

Zine's op-ed continued:

> *As an academic, I support free speech as well as academic freedom. But these are not without limitations. Freedom of expression is limited by the consequences of that speech. Spreading hate is not free speech.*

It turns out that fear-mongering about free speech was Zine's shtick. In an article titled "The alt-right and the weaponization of free speech on campus" in Academic Matters, she wrote:

> *...I want to address growing concerns about neofascism and white supremacy on campuses and how the so-called alt-right are weaponizing free speech and using it as a rhetorical prop in campaigns of ideological intimidation. These groups engage in tactics of vandalism, harassment, and intimidation under the cover of a "free speech" alibi.*
>
> *Sacrificing human rights on the altar of free speech has become a strategy in the alt-right toolkit of bigotry. Newly emboldened neofascist groups are*

coming out from the shadows of internet chatrooms and entering the public sphere. This includes a more prominent presence at our universities.[67]

And what was Zine's evidence of these claims? A handful of "It's OK To Be White" posters put up at a few Canadian universities. Zine then said that pro-free speech activists are deploying "spies in classrooms" to monitor professors.

During my MA research proposal presentation, Zine used the allotted question period to vocalize the same opinions she wrote in those op-eds. I scanned the room as she continued lecturing me about hate speech and Holocaust denial and white supremacy and Islamophobic bigotry: every single one of my classmates was looking down at their feet. My MA supervisor never jumped in to intervene – it would have been nice if he had said something like "How about we get back on track" or "Maybe we could see if someone else had questions for Lindsay?" but he looked as uncomfortable as everyone else. I didn't hold it against him. Yet even as Zine and the other professor were trying to humiliate me in front of my entire department, I didn't care. I was in a very different state of mind than I was a few months ago, when I had cried during the meeting with Nathan Rambukkana, Herbert Pimlott, and Adria Joel. Now, I simply nodded and smiled politely as I listened to her paranoid tirade about alt-right Holocaust-denying white supremacist neo-fascist free speech.

*

Just as with the previous semester, the campus environment was alienating, but the rest of my life was going quite swimmingly.

In March, while at UC Berkeley, I had dinner at the Faculty Club, where I was seated next to Harvard political philosophy professor Harvey Mansfield, who later sent me a couple of books that he had written or translated. My family then met me down in San Francisco, where we hung out all day at Pier 39, and I did triple flips on the bungee trampoline.

I learned that a Timmins, Ontario high school student named Aidan Buhler won first prize in the A&E "Lives That Make a Difference Essay Contest" after writing about me. Her essay was chosen out of over 1,000 entries. As reported in the Timmins Daily Press:[68]

> *Sara Hinzman, vice-president for distribution with A&E Networks, said, "Aidan's essay eloquently captured the central role the actions Lindsay Shepherd had on igniting discussion on gender identity and free speech in Canada in 2018."*
>
> *"Her essay depicted the value of a diversity of opinions and perspectives in Canada's institutions of higher education."*
>
> *"Aidan's essay focused on Lindsay Shepherd's influence, writing that she 'brought to light the important issues of freedom of speech and freedom of inquiry within the learning environment.'" She explained her impact on Canada and how "the issues raised by Lindsay Shepherd's experience help Canadians understand the value of their educational institutions and the importance of free academic inquiry."*

My heart swelled with happiness for Aidan, and I was honoured that she had written about me.

I found out I would be presented with two awards in the upcoming months: in May, the 2018 Harry Weldon Canadian Values Award, from the Peace, Order, and Good Government think tank; and in June, the 2018 Outstanding Graduate Student Award from Heterodox Academy. I had also confirmed a mid-August speaking engagement in Australia.

I was getting the opportunity to meet with accomplished academics, authors, and professionals; I was travelling and doing speaking engagements; and I had even won two awards. All that was much more important than fretting about what catty classmates, snide professors, and angry Rainbow Centre activists thought about me.

On April 24, 2018, Laurier's Task Force on Freedom of Expression was hosting a townhall to present the institutional statement on freedom of expression they had written. There was no filming allowed inside, which was unfortunate, as it was quite the event. CTV showed up but was ordered to leave the room.

The task force's Statement on Freedom of Expression was long and winding – its authors had clearly tried to appease both free speech advocates and diversity zealots.

> *Laurier recognizes that at times free expression may harm and/or further marginalize community members from visible and invisible minority groups, including, but not limited to those from groups based on Indigeneity, class, race, ethnicity, place of origin, religious creed, spiritual belief, sexual orientation, gender identity and expression, age, and ability. In such cases, the university encourages its community members to respond with an educational and intellectual approach that increases awareness and consideration of diverse positions. The university reaffirms its commitment to creating an inclusive environment for all Laurier community members, and to providing access to services that support well-being and safety from physical harm.*

> *Some challenging cases of free expression will have to be navigated, but it is not the role of the university to censor speech. To grant the institution such power would set a dangerous precedent. Even if institutional censorship were deemed acceptable in one context, there is no guarantee that such restriction would be applied fairly or wisely in other contexts, or as power changes hands over time. Rather than restricting speech, Laurier is committed to supporting an open and inclusive environment that also protects free expression. Community members are free to reject and vigorously contest ideas while still recognizing the right to express or hear those ideas. The university aspires for its community to engage in better speech whereby members strive for a high ethical and intellectual standard for open and constructive discourse.[69]*

I regarded the idea of a Statement on Freedom of Expression as superfluous: if such a statement was going to exist, all it needed to do was affirm the university's historical and philosophical commitment to open inquiry and free discussion, and reiterate that the only limits to free speech are already laid out in the Criminal Code.

When the Q&A portion of the townhall kicked off, after the task force presented their Statement, the first person to approach the microphone was a male student who immediately accused the panel of producing a document that "upholds white supremacy."[70]

Prof. Ali Zaidi, a task force member, leaned into his microphone and replied, "How *dare* you call me a white supremacist," to some light applause in the audience.

Task force member Prof. David Haskell then described social conservatives and Christians as the most marginalized groups on university campuses today, which caused an audience member, perhaps the same one who accused the panel of white supremacy, to heckle: "You are a terrible person!"

Toby from the Rainbow Centre then emotionally recited a spoken-word poem about the harms of free speech, and how he had a "broken body." Toby then performatively hugged Milas, who was standing behind Toby for support, and they embraced for a long time, still at the microphone, before Toby ran to the back of the room and burst his way out of the doors.

Funnily enough, a couple weeks later, I was sitting on the bus going to campus, sitting in the seat closest to the window of a two-seater section, when I saw Milas walk up the steps and slip into the extra seat right beside me. I suspect Milas at some point realized they were sitting beside me, because they turned to look out the window and then did a double-take after glancing in my direction. There were a few empty seats further back, but Milas didn't move. Milas was one of the people who had been publicly denouncing me as a scary transphobe who is threatening lives and denying existences, but here they were, sitting right beside me on the bus.

I had very little in common with Toby and Milas worldview-wise, but they were willing to put their faces and names out there to speak out for what they believed in, which was far more respectable than cowering away and staying silent.

Upon the conclusion of the town hall, CTV was outside and they asked me for an interview. I told them exactly what I thought: would this institutional Statement on Freedom of Expression have prevented the situation I found myself in after playing the TVO clip? No. There was still a Sexual Violence policy that claimed open discussion about pronouns was gendered harassment, and there was still an entire diversity and inclusion apparatus to enforce such policies.

CHAPTER 17

A week or so after the townhall, I was hitching a ride to Ottawa, where I was going to speak on a panel about free expression at the city's public library organized by the Humanist Association of Ottawa. I was slouching in the back of the car, idly scrolling through my phone and sipping my Tim Hortons coffee.

I shot straight up upon seeing I had a new email from the Senior Advisor of Dispute Resolution and Support at Wilfrid Laurier University.

"What now?" I said aloud to myself.

The advisor, Dawn McDermott, wrote to me:

> *Hi Lindsay, As indicated below I am the Senior Advisor of Dispute Resolution and Support. I need to connect with you with regard to a formal harassment complaint that has been filed in my office, naming you as the respondent. For your review, I have attached a link to Laurier's Prevention of Discrimination and Harassment Policy.*
>
> *Would you be available to meet in my office tomorrow at 10:30 AM or 1:30 PM? I also have some availability on Monday morning. Please let me know what works best for you.*

I replied instantly, writing that I was available Monday, but would appreciate some details in the meantime.

"Sure," Dawn wrote back. "Ethan Jackson has filed a formal complaint of harassment under policy 6.1. I will share the complaint with you on Monday and we can discuss the process."

Ethan Jackson? The person who made a speech at the Trans Solidarity Rally saying "violence is okay," organized a protest against LSOI's Faith

Goldy event, posted countless social media comments about me, and tried to force me to leave the printing room?

How curious was it that Ethan chose to file the complaint against me when the last term of classes had already concluded. Graduate students did not have on-campus classes in the summer: our major research papers were completed remotely and independently, and we would graduate from our 12-month programs in late August. He knew he would never have to encounter me again, but made a complaint anyways.

I skimmed Policy 6.1, Prevention of Harassment and Discrimination. It read, in part:

> *Where harassing or discriminatory behaviours are severe and/or pervasive and cause unreasonable interference with a person's study or work environment, a poisoned environment may be created. A poisoned work or learning environment is one that is intimidating, hostile and/or offensive. A poisoned environment can arise from even a single incident. It may be created by the comments or actions of any person, regardless of his or her status. The comments or conduct do not have to be directed at a particular individual. A person need not be the target of the behaviours to feel the effects of certain harassing and/or discriminatory behaviours at their place of work or study.*

The policy expressly stated that cases of "interpersonal conflict or disagreement" did not constitute harassment.

My understanding of university complaint processes – corroborated by my research into complaint processes at other Canadian universities – seemed to be that informal resolution and mediation was attempted before a complaint escalated into a full-fledged investigation.

When I sat down in Dawn's office on Monday, I asked her why Ethan's complaint had gone straight to an investigation rather than mediation.

"The policy allows for there to be an informal resolution if there is an appetite on the part of the parties. That generally includes mediation, facilitated dialogue. Ethan has said absolutely not, he is not prepared to engage in mediation. That means that he is requesting the complaint be moved to an investigation," Dawn informed Prof. Haskell and I in the meeting, which I recorded with permission. Prof. Haskell had come along with me to retrieve the complaint and convince Dawn that any previous interactions I had with Ethan did not meet the threshold of harassment, and that this was a case of mutual dislike and disagreement. Dawn was not convinced.

Of course Ethan didn't want to go to mediation – the whole purpose of the complaint was to try to get me in trouble, not to solve our mutual disagreements and become amicable with one another.

Dawn informed me that the investigation would proceed whether or not I participated, and said that if I am found in violation of the Harassment and Discrimination policy, the possible consequences could include not having any contact with Ethan (fine by me); having a letter on my file; or even being expelled, though she hadn't seen that happen before. Even though she said she hadn't seen anyone expelled, I suspected that the university administrators would happily make an exception for me. Nevertheless, as author Mark Steyn has said, "The eventual verdict is largely irrelevant: The process is the punishment."[71]

I was sent away with a hard copy of Ethan's four-page typed-out complaint. About 10-15% of it was redacted, with swaths of blacked out text.

The complaint began:

> *I, Ethan Jackson, am alleging that Lindsay Shepherd (LS) has harassed me on campus and online which has led to a poisoned work and study environment.*

What vegan [sic] in October 2017 in LS' role as Teaching Assistant sparked a rise in tension within the faculty of Arts on campus. This rise in tension was evident in classrooms beginning November 2017, which ultimately put an onus on queer and trans faculty and students to call for safety and security measures, and supports to be put in place for our well-being… What LS has done is a pattern of harassment and intimidation though a series of events. LS' actions have culminated a pattern of direct and indirect forms of discrimination on the basis of my transgender identity.

Already, a spelling error and a timeline discrepancy – the semester had started in September and the controversy was sparked in November.

Ethan proceeded with a timeline covering the incidents where I had allegedly harassed him between November 2017 and March 2018.

He first accused me of doxxing – "doxxing" being the public release of peoples' private phone numbers, addresses, family members' names, and the like. Ethan was using a very, shall we say, *liberal* definition of doxxing: all I had done was reply to some of his tweets and point out that he was a graduate student colleague of mine, a fact that was already apparent from his own social media activity. It seemed that he was permitted to tweet at me and tag me in tweets as much as he pleased, but if I took the bait and replied, I was doxxing him. Ethan is trans, which means talking back to him is violence.

The document continued:

December 19th: I emailed [redacted] about my safety concerns, and that I was feeling uncomfortable, unsafe, and mentally and emotionally exhausted from balancing work. I did not want to return to WLU because of the growing tension and harassment online by LS' platform and followers. I was fearful because I knew that LS was going to be in one of my CS [Communication Studies] classes, CS617: Risk Media and Science in Winter 2018.

Interesting: he had known, prior to any class list being released, that I was going to be in his class the following semester. I hadn't any idea who was going to be in my classes. Looks like he and the professor of that course, Penelope Ironstone, were close friends.

> *I was worried and keeping faculty members and superiors informed of my mental and emotional state because of LS' presence... They supported me through the term and let me submit my final assignments the day before Winter 2018 term began.*

> *January 2018: I decided to return to class because I belong here. However, come January has meant CS617 would be a challenge to navigate because I would share a class with LS. It was very tense.*

Of course, even in a formal harassment complaint, Ethan couldn't help but include his self-affirming mantras about how he "belongs here." As for his assertion that "it was very tense" – was it? I recalled feeling in that Communication Studies class that everyone was making the effort to be civil, and that there was surprisingly no detectable tension.

> *It was incredibly difficult because LS was always on her phone, giving me the impression she was on social media, but was disengaged from participation. I was afraid that if I would say something, she would post these things from the classroom online.*

I hooted. There was some truth to his observation: I was often distracted by my phone and laptop in class because I had an endless mound of emails to answer, requests to respond to, and opportunities to gauge. It was a busy time in my life, and I sometimes wished I had a personal assistant to help me get through my inbox. But in the world Ethan had created in his head, my whole life's purpose was to harass him, so if I was on my phone, it must be because I was talking about him. It even sounded like he was trying to snitch on me to get my participation marks docked, even though I had already graduated from that class with an A-.

He then wrote a paragraph complaining that my Twitter followers were mean to him, saying "LS continued to allow the hate and harassment to go viral," as if I were the grand arbiter of Twitter. He continued:

> *January 17 2018: …I went back to my CS graduate lab to retrieve my laptop and bag. LS was in this lab using the CS printer – a place she should not be in – she is not in CS but in CAST. As I was gathering my things, I asked LS what she was doing there as this isn't a space for CAST students… I tried to leave to which she said a few things under her breath. I asked her what she said. She said she called me "petty and pathetic." To which I turned and left. [redacted]. As a result of this, I emailed several administrators and faculty to report this bullying… I no longer felt safe in my own classes, let alone on campus.*
>
> *January 18 2018–January 28 2018: My studying environment was therefore hostile and toxic enough that I could not attend without additional accommodation to ensure my safety and encouragement to engage in course material.*

The basis of Ethan's complaint was that I had harassed him because he is transgender. But halfway through the complaint, there was still no indication that I attacked his transgender identity in any way.

He then described how he arranged to work one-on-one with Professor Ironstone rather than coming into class, as he could not endure being in the same room as me for the CS617 class. It was interesting that Professor Ironstone had agreed to tutor him one-on-one.

> *I continued to be aware of growing harassment and the ways I would constantly "run into" LS in the same halls and stairwells.*

I suppose he put "run into" in quotation marks to imply I was stalking him. He and I were both graduate students in the Faculty of Arts, and TAs in the same departments, on a small campus. I don't even remember ever passing by him in the hallways or stairwells, but I'm sure it was a probable occurrence, given the circumstances.

> *[redacted name] suggested I change the location of my Teaching Assistant tutorial room because LS and I taught Friday mornings 8:30am-10:20am in the same building, floors apart. I needed further accommodation to separate myself from LS because of the growing awareness of her presence around me and the lack of address from administration.*

The final incident he laid out was in March 2018. He described how my club, LSOI, invited Faith Goldy to speak on campus. He started off by talking about how he was petrified to see me in a hallway accompanied by "two large men," affixing LSOI event promotion posters to the walls and bulletin boards (I was accompanied by two LSOI members, who I would say are reasonably-sized people).

> *When I turned the corner, I noticed that they were all standing at the other end of the hall, near the CS department cork board… I did not feel safe to return to my office as I was caught in the hallway and did not want to turn my back to the three. I immediately turned right and used the stairwell in DAWB to leave and find a second person because I did not feel safe to be alone.*

Ethan then described how me and my two large henchmen ran around chasing him up and down the halls, terrorizing him and filming him with "video cameras."

In reality, Ethan was ripping down all of the posters we had put up, so we were re-tracing the areas where they had been taken down, and we wanted to catch any video evidence of the posters being ripped down. I wasn't worried about the Laurier investigator believing Ethan's account, as I assumed they would have security camera footage of the hallways, which would show no such manhunt occurred.

Next, Ethan came across another poster that apparently bothered him. The Diversity and Equity Office affiliates had put up posters around campus that read "Brown Lives Matter / Black Lives Matter / Indigenous Lives Matter / Queer Lives Matter / Trans Lives Matter / Migrant Lives Matter," and though it was irrelevant to his complaint against me, Ethan wanted to describe, in his complaint, coming across one such poster that had some added graffiti:

> *I noticed that one of the posters on the wall had "white lives matter" written on it… I needed to report that, as this is a direct violation and a racist statement… this needed to be brought back to the DEO [Diversity and Equity Office].*

He concluded:

> *I do not feel safe on campus alone - I am in constant contact with friends and supports if I am on campus to know that I have someone on the other end if anything comes up… I must stay in public spaces where others are in case there is anything that happens, I cannot be left alone because of LS and her actions that have poisoned what was once a safer spaces [sic] for me. My academics and my drive for research and thriving within academia is suffering because of the toxic environment that LS poisoned for me based off of these recurring actions of harassment and intimidation. I am afraid of what will happen next because of these escalating patterns of targeting me.*

I spoke with the investigator hired by the university in May 2018, and gave my input on Ethan's complaint. I mentioned to the dispute resolution coordinator, Dawn McDermott, that I was writing my major research paper over the summer, and didn't want this complaint to be looming over me, as it would interfere with my focus. Deep down, I was also worried that perhaps there would be no point in me spending the summer writing my paper, as they were going to use this complaint to expel me or somehow thwart the completion of my MA.

But Dawn assured me that the whole matter would be resolved within 48 hours of my meeting with the investigator.

In the meantime, I had an important event to host.

*

I had only exchanged a couple of brief emails with Dr. Frances Widdowson before meeting her in London, Ontario at the annual meeting of the Society for Academic Freedom and Scholarship. Dr. Widdowson, a professor at Calgary's Mount Royal University in the Department of Economics, Justice, and Policy Studies, was one of the only academics in Canada willing to critically question university indigenization initiatives. She was also the first academic I was aware of who sounded the alarm on land acknowledgments, arguing:[72]

> ...there is nothing wrong with individuals making political statements recognizing indigenous peoples' traditional territory. It is a mistake, however, for a university to make official declarations that assume that all faculty, staff and students agree with these pronouncements. If universities are going to make these statements, they should expect that dissenters will also publicly oppose these assertions when declarations are made on their behalf. By leaving these declarations up to individuals, honest positions, rather than coerced hollow gestures, can be expressed.

Dr. Widdowson has pointed out that initiatives such as university-mandated indigenous course content and the institutional promotion of indigenous "knowledge systems" threaten open inquiry and undermine dedication to the scientific method. If an instructor or student is ordered to unquestioningly respect "indigenous ways of knowing," critical thinking is in turn discouraged. "Indigenization advocates try to intimidate intellectual challengers with accusations of 'racism' and 'colonialism.' There are even arguments that the refutation of any indigenous idea constitutes 'epistemological racism' or, more astonishingly, 'epistemicide,'" Dr. Widdowson has argued. "This pressure has a negative impact on open inquiry; it creates an emotional 'no-go zone' that is hostile to examining indigenous-non-indigenous relations rationally. While this will increase the power of indigenization advocates and the resources made available to them, it will not improve indigenous education."

Dr. Widdowson was ultimately advocating for equal opportunity of education for both non-indigenous and indigenous populations: "Educational achievement can only be improved if people are better able to understand the world around them, and this is not facilitated by many indigenization initiatives," she has written.

LSOI arranged for Dr. Widdowson to speak at Laurier on the topic of "Does University Indigenization Threaten Open Inquiry?" on May 9, 2018. Weeks after Prof. McNally submitted our room request, we finally got a response from the university. On May 2, 2018 at 4:32pm, the university announced a new policy: all event-related security fees from that point forward must be paid by the event organizer, and nothing will be covered by the university. At 4:45pm, they emailed LSOI, letting us know the security cost for Dr. Widdowson's talk would be $5,473.

I could be persuaded that in some circumstances, a small security fee might be justified. But it was preposterous for a university to charge a student group $5,473 in security fees to bring a Canadian university professor to another Canadian university campus, in order to share knowledge and research. The reason for the exorbitant security quote – if not conjured up solely to deter us from hosting the event – was a protest event planned by the local Antifa clubs, "Racists Aren't Welcome Here."[73]

"We cannot condone LSOI's repeated efforts to spread their openly white supremacist agenda. These actions are a destructive force in our community. Hate cannot have a platform," the Facebook event page read.

Laurier had burdened LSOI with thousands of dollars in security costs so that a group of angry, masked misfits could protest our event. If anyone should be paying for these fees, it should have been the protesters.

The LSOI executive members mulled it over, and we decided we should try to fundraise as much of the $5,473 fee as we could. And in less than 48 hours, we did it: we had surpassed the amount quoted to us by the university, just by pleading our case on Twitter.[74] I was fortunate that I had the profile that allowed the cause to gain publicity: there were surely many organizations and groups that had faced the same circumstances, but had no means of gathering the funds. We were also fortunate that people understood the importance of this talk and were willing to chip in to make it happen. Part of our fundraising page read:

> *Two Antifa groups in the Kitchener-Waterloo region have planned a protest for Dr. Widdowson's talk. We completely respect their plans to protest, so long as Dr. Widdowson's talk is not overly disrupted or shut down. However, the name of the protest, "Racists Aren't Welcome Here," unfortunately indicates that open inquiry is indeed threatened on our campuses — some people deem the topic of indigenization simply too touchy and taboo, and anyone who dares to address this topic is "racist." While some were quick to label Dr. Widdowson as a racist right-winger, and LSOI President Lindsay Shepherd as a white supremacist sympathizer and LSOI as an alt-right apologist club, we will kindly point out that Dr. Widdowson is a Marxist-socialist. Labels like "racist" and "white supremacist" too often needlessly stifle open inquiry and perpetuate misinformation.*

> *Your donation would be of great service to free speech and open inquiry in Canada, as we see it as a problem that only certain speakers who are deemed too controversial by radical leftist activists will cost extra security fees, which means anyone who wants to hear someone with a non-politically correct view will likely have to pay a ticket price, whereas politically correct events can be free. We want to make Dr. Widdowson's talk free for anyone who wants to attend.*

It was not only Waterloo's revolutionary communist groups that were opposed to Dr. Widdowson's presence: some Wilfrid Laurier University officials were so appalled by the idea that Dr. Widdowson could question the legitimacy of indigenization initiatives that they organized a counter-event at the same time as her talk. The Wilfrid Laurier University Faculty Association (WLUFA) released a statement that said "The WLUFA executive recognizes that recent actions by the Laurier Society for Open Inquiry are not, in fact, promoting intellectual debate on our university campuses, but seem instead to be manufacturing a free speech 'crisis' at Laurier where none exists."[75]

That's right: to the faculty association executives, a professor giving a speech at a university on an academic topic with social currency apparently does not promote intellectual debate on a university campus. And according to these professors, the fact that this talk cost over $5,000 in security fees was no cause for concern. Nothing to see here, move along.

President Deborah MacLatchy then sent an email to faculty and staff reiterating Laurier's total and complete dedication to freedom of expression; but the email also conveniently mentioned that at the exact same time as the Widdowson talk, there was another event people could attend: the "Gathering of Good Minds" pipe ceremony, hosted by WLU's Office of Indigenous Initiatives. The pipe ceremony was organized as a "healing space" to "affirm Indigenization," according to WLU's Senior Adviser of Indigenous Initiatives.[76] MacLatchy also emailed out the link to a new crowdfunding campaign: the "Indigenous Knowledge Fund," which Professor of Indigenous Studies Lianne Leddy set up directly in response to the Widdowson event.[77]

While universities may let a "controversial" event go ahead, it will not be done without (1) charging the host group thousands in security fees; (2) diverting attention away from the original event by creating another one at the exact same time promoting the opposing view (meaning that attendees will have to choose to attend one event or the other, making it impossible to explore both sides); and (3) pushing a campaign that is raising money for the precise issue that the guest speaker is challenging. The appropriate disavowals are also required before the "controversial" event can go ahead: Laurier's Office of Indigenous Initiatives released a statement on their official website saying that the Office "does not endorse the May 9 event featuring Frances Widdowson and we are strongly opposed to her views on Indigenization."[78]

*

On May 9, we arrived at the campus to see the building and front parking lots surrounded by fences, gates, and blockading materials, as if an international celebrity or foreign dignitary were about to descend upon the campus. Security guards were stationed throughout the entire building, and a bag search and ID check was set up at the door. Notably, it was May, meaning the regular September-April academic year had concluded and most students had gone home for the summer. The campus was deserted. But still, we were expecting a healthy attendance of 40 people.

Dr. Widdowson pulled up to the Bricker Academic Building, and as we were greeting one another, we started to hear a distant chanting, increasing in volume. We spotted a large red banner and a horde of protesters marching down towards us. "One Solution: Revolution," the banner read. Another one became visible: "Workers Unite Against the Far-Right! Fight back Against Fascism!" The bottom of the banner read "www.marxist.ca." The protesters, equipped with megaphones, were chanting "When indigenous lives are under attack, what do we do? Stand up, fight back!" and "Trans Rights are Human Rights!"

We later found out that the Socialist Fightback campus network had carpooled in their entire southern Ontario membership to the protest.[79]

"Do you even know what you're protesting? Why don't you see what Dr. Widdowson actually has to say?" I hollered at the protesters. But any time you tried to communicate with them, they only chanted louder, to drown you out. One female protester blared an airhorn at anyone who addressed the protesters. At one point, when they chanted about how the working class must rise up, Dr. Widdowson, a leftist herself, yelled back at them, "I agree with you!" But they yelled over her with their megaphones and drowned her out with the air horns. Right before going into the room when the event was about to start, a tall male protester, with sunglasses and a bandana covering his face, came up to me and yelled in my face, "Everybody fucking hates you, Lindsay."

Dr. Widdowson introduced her talk by noting:

> ...I'm a socialist as well, which is totally ironic, I went out and tried to talk to the protesters, and said hey, I agree with your signs here! We are in agreement, it's just that we don't seem to be understanding each other very well, so why don't you come in, hear the talk, and maybe we can reach a better understanding of what's going on and why I think that indigenization is a serious problem for universities in general, but it is a serious problem especially for indigenous students... the actual anti-indigenous people are all the lawyers and consultants who are all making the money off of initiatives like indigenization which are just terribly thought-out, anti-intellectual, destructive to education generally, but especially destructive to education for indigenous students.

Widdowson discussed how indigenization initiatives are anti-science, and how the stifling of open inquiry on these topics does not come from only left-wingers, but from what she termed "politically correct totalitarians" that can come from any political or ideological stripe.

"We want to improve circumstances for indigenous people! How will indigenization do that? It won't do it!" she said.

When the event concluded, the protest was still going on outside, even though night had fallen. The group continued their chanting for a short while, but a large chunk of the herd took off, leaving only 20 or so of the more militant masked folks. The smaller group then began chanting, repeatedly, "Fuck you, Lindsay," but in a sing-songy way: "Fuuuuuccckkk youuuuu, Liiiinnnndsay." I was right beside them as they chanted – I didn't feel physically threatened. I was actually kind of flattered.

"Fuck you, Lindsay," they chanted, swaying back and forth. Toby from the Rainbow Centre was amongst them, but not chanting, and looking sheepish. "Fuck you, Lindsay," they continued. I scanned the crowd to see which unmasked individuals I could identify remaining at the protest: I recognized a couple Laurier PhD students, including Kira Williams, the trans advocate who had been interviewed in Maclean's.

I would later come across a PowerPoint presentation Kira made after speaking on a panel called "Trans Equity: Current Issues and Events in Ontario's Universities," where they brought up the Laurier affair as a case study. Kira's first bullet point said "In November 2017, Lindsay Shepherd played Dr. Jordan Peterson making hateful remarks against trans people in a first-year course." Another bullet point said "Shepherd continued her agitation in the past year against trans students."

I asked Kira, over Twitter, what "hateful remarks" Peterson had said in the TVO clip, and how I had "continued agitating trans students." Kira would never get around to answering me – these people never do when you ask them directly for evidence. They believe that the act of you asking for evidence is proof of your transphobia, as you are piling onto a trans person and subjecting them to harassment by targeting their (public) Twitter account. One of Kira's next PowerPoint slides said "Because of these events at Laurier, trans people like me have experienced: Concerns for and attacks on our physical safety and well-being while on campus" and "Narratives invisibilising our existence and implying it as problematic to issues of 'free speech.'"[80]

As the last few protesters chased LSOI event attendees around with air horns, blared siren machines in our ears, and swore at us, the LSOI team and I called it a night, and went to the bar, where Dr. Widdowson and some of the faculty members and attendees were already seated.

*

That coming weekend, I was going to be accepting the 2018 Harry Weldon Canadian Values Award in Ottawa. The Frances Widdowson event was successfully completed, and in the end, Laurier only charged LSOI $5,332 instead of $5,473 in security fees – lucky us. I sat back in my seat on the VIA Rail train and stared out onto the plains of Southern Ontario. I could now think more about the complaint lodged against me by Ethan Jackson. The whole thing reeked of collusion. Why did the dispute resolution office accept a complaint about me at the tail-end of the regular academic year, when I wouldn't even be taking classes on the campus anymore, and was on track to graduate within months? On the train, I got back in touch with Howard Levitt, the star lawyer who had been giving me advice throughout the affair and had asked me a couple times whether I wanted to sue. I updated him about this newest development. When he asked me again if I would consider legal action against Laurier, this time, I said yes.

In legalese, my statement of claim against Nathan Rambukkana, Herbert Pimlott, Adria Joel, and Wilfrid Laurier University alleged harassment, intentional infliction of nervous shock, negligence, and constructive dismissal, claiming damages of $3.6 million.

"Although Pimlott, Rambukkana and Joel had acted recklessly, maliciously and in bad faith, and it was ultimately determined by the University that this meeting should have never occurred, no action has been taken by the University against them and Shepherd was provided no protection from their predations," my claim read.

The Wilfrid Laurier Faculty Association (WLUFA), in response to the news of the lawsuit, said:[81]

> *As the legal rigmarole intensifies, the Association will work to keep attention focused on the following three principles that we believe are important to our community:*
>
> 1. *The academic freedom of the two faculty members who expressed their views about Ms. Shepherd's conduct in a tutorial she led;*
> 2. *The fact that a course instructor is responsible for the content of a course, has academic freedom in teaching, and has an obligation to supervise and, if necessary, correct the conduct of teaching assistants hired to assist with their courses;*
> 3. *The responsibility of the University for the actions of its managers and the defence of its own policies.*

No, no, no. The trio hadn't merely "expressed their views" about my "conduct," but had invented complaints to dangle over my head and accused me of violating provincial and federal law. I suppose that is how you "correct the conduct" of a TA who doesn't abide by the radical leftist academic agenda. I fully respected the principle of academic freedom, and if Rambukkana had pulled me aside back in November 2017 and told me he doesn't want the issue of pronouns discussed in his course, I would have understood and abided by his wishes. But that wasn't what he did.

There had been no issue with my conduct: Wilfrid Laurier University had already said in their December 18, 2017 release regarding the independent fact-finder's report, "There was no wrongdoing on the part of Ms. Shepherd in showing the clip from TVO in her tutorial. Showing a TVO clip for the purposes of an academic discussion is a reasonable classroom teaching tool… We have no reason to believe this discussion was not handled well in the tutorial in question."

With the same lawyer, Howard Levitt, Jordan Peterson also launched a suit against Rambukkana, Pimlott, Joel, and Laurier, for defamation. In turn, Laurier commenced a third party claim against me, arguing that if Jordan Peterson was indeed defamed by Rambukkana, Pimlott, and Joel, it would be my fault for recording their remarks, and it would be me who would be responsible for paying out any damages to Peterson.

As I'm sure is the case with many plaintiffs, I had some apprehension toward involving the courts, but ultimately, thought it might set an interesting precedent that could tell us a lot about the future of free expression rights and the role of the university. If I was awarded any money, I pledged to donate to organizations fighting for free speech on campus, such as the Justice Centre for Constitutional Freedoms, Heterodox Academy, and the Society for Academic Freedom and Scholarship.

Alas, I was warned that the lawsuit would move at a glacial pace, which is indeed the case, at the time of writing.

CHAPTER 18

The summer of 2018 was beautiful in Waterloo. My boyfriend (now husband) Cosmin and I spent our days bicycling around the city. Uptown Waterloo had just installed bike lanes, which were apparently quite controversial, but I made use of them often. Cosmin was taking summer courses and I was writing my MA paper, so we would meet at a cafe everyday to work on our assignments together. In June, I was flown to LA to film a segment for the American documentary film "No Safe Spaces," and later in the month I was invited to speak at ideacity 2018, a conference reminiscent of TED founded by Toronto media mogul Moses Znaimer. Cosmin and I stayed in Toronto for half a week, at a hotel in Yorkville. After delivering my speech at the grandiose Koerner Hall, I went backstage to get de-microphoned in the green room, and another speaker in the lounge said to me, "Nice speech, I was a bit surprised. I thought you were some sort of neocon." Cosmin and I drank wine at the opening night party at Casa Loma, a Gothic Revival style mansion, and schmoozed at the closing night party at the Zoomerplex over Neapolitan pizza and cocktails.

The Ontario provincial election was also that June, and I was invited to work on the campaign for a local Progressive Conservative candidate, door-knocking and dropping literature in mailboxes. I also joined the electoral district association board of the Kitchener South—Hespeler federal Conservatives. My membership with the Green Party had expired many months ago, so when they called me and asked if I wanted to renew and donate, I answered, "Sorry, I joined a different party."

"May I ask which one?" the fundraiser asked me.

"Yes. The Conservatives," I replied.

"The Conservatives? My, that's… quite a change," he said.

"Yes," I said. "It is."

"Okay, well, then… goodbye."

I chuckled when I imagined telling my 18-year-old self that in five years, I would be working with the Conservatives. I was even approached by several party officials who wanted me to run as a candidate in the 2019 election. At the start of the Laurier affair, I had been defensive about being called a conservative, and made sure to correct people that I most certainly wasn't one. But a few months down the road, I stopped caring about what people labelled me, and it didn't bother me when people called me conservative, even though I didn't think it was a wholly accurate label.

I entertained running for office. The Conservatives sent me a nomination package, and I started filling it out, though I was still torn.

"I don't really feel like I fit in with the Conservative Party. I don't really think I'm a conservative," I told Laurier professor David Haskell, who had also been approached by the party to stand as a candidate.

"Well, there are Red Tories and Blue Tories," he told me. "You would be a Red Tory."

Ultimately, I abandoned my application. I never completed the paperwork, and the party never chased after me. I was just finding my footing as someone who championed free expression and independent thought, and the idea of publicly representing a political party seemed like it would be too stifling.

I had dabbled in only one previous political endeavour – an unpaid internship at the Burnaby North—Seymour Liberal constituency office in 2016. I lived only a 10-minute bike ride away from the office, so I would whiz down Hastings Street on my pastel purple Norco bike to get there.

The staff at the office were nice, I suppose, but some struck me as insincere. Around the time of Chinese New Year, I was stuffing and sealing hundreds of little red envelopes with candy when one of the staff said to me with a childish grin, "Here at this office, we *love* Chinese people! And most of all, we love all the Chinese restaurants they open!"

I winced.

At least I got a nice reference letter at the end, which I used to win a scholarship at SFU. Otherwise, that Liberal office didn't even have the basic decency to provide the unpaid volunteers with a carafe of coffee.

I remember sorting through the office's mail one day, and coming across a letter written by a constituent who was gently urging the MP, Terry Beech, to prioritize homeless and low-income Canadians over Syrian refugees (this was in 2016, when Syrian refugees were all the rage), making the point that the Liberals were abandoning their own citizens. I read the letter, and thought to myself, *this guy kind of has a point.* I wasn't opposed to Canada taking in refugees, but I hadn't ever heard a critical viewpoint expressed before. I showed my supervisor the letter to see what he would say about it.

"Yeah, unfortunately we sometimes get mail from people like that," he said, shaking his head.

I looked back at the letter, and had one of those pangs where you realize one of your thoughts or opinions is unacceptable to someone else. If I were to express out loud that I thought the letter made some good points, I would have been shunned. Those pangs are what make you realize that you'd be better off staying quiet about certain things.

*

The candidate I worked for in the 2018 Ontario election, Progressive Conservative Amy Fee, ended up winning her riding, as did another local candidate, over in Kitchener Centre: Laura Mae Lindo. Lindo was the director of the Wilfrid Laurier University Diversity & Equity Office who went on leave and ran for the provincial NDP. Her platform championed diversity and representation – she was a part of the new wave of professionals who base their careers off of their identity and insist that they should fill high-powered positions for the purposes of "representation." Rather than emphasize their policy positions, skills, or accomplishments, they insisted their identity was the reason they should be selected for a job.

"Little girls need to see someone like me in government, so they know they can grow up to be a politician too," they'll say.

When Lindo was elected to the legislature, she said to the media, "I think I might be the first person to ever have dreads at Queen's Park." She claimed that as a woman of colour, she "had never felt the building would be a place [she] could work," omitting the fact that her uncle was a former cabinet minister.

Lindo told The Record that she had "never listened" to the Laurier recording that thrust her office into the national spotlight.[82] I found that, at best, hard to believe: she really didn't have an ounce of interest in investigating why her own staff member and her own university office was being blasted all over the Canadian and international news, not to mention social media and YouTube? I didn't buy it. I reckoned she was simply trying to distance herself from that monster of a department she had led.

*

I checked my school email every single day over the summer, anticipating a decision about the harassment and discrimination complaint lodged against me. Dawn had told me in early May that they would have the investigation done in 48 hours, but June and July had now flown by.

In August, I flew down to Australia to speak for a conference organized by the Centre for Independent Studies. For the first time in my life, I was flying first class. I had my laptop open in my first-class pod, equipped with a relatively large TV, ample storage space, and a desk area I was using to finish up my master's paper, which was due in a few hours. I would be submitting my paper while in the air, via the plane's Wi-Fi, and defending my paper once I was back in Waterloo in a couple weeks.

The flight attendant came around and brought me a sweet potato, ginger, and cardamom soup, and a main course of green vegetable curry with herbed rice. I was then offered a dessert or cheese plate and espresso, of which I only accepted the espresso. I was terrified of such a long nighttime voyage over the vast Pacific Ocean, but figured that if we crashed, at least I would die in first class.

After finishing my espresso and reading a couple chapters of Douglas Murray's *The Strange Death of Europe*, I pressed the button to convert my seat into a full-length bed and pulled up the comforter. I had one of the best sleeps of my life. When I awoke, everyone else was still snoozing and the plane was still dark, so I meandered to the front of the Virgin Atlantic plane. When I pulled back the curtain at the front of the aisle, I saw a full bar area, with barstools around the counter, lit with a purplish-blue LED glow. You could walk around freely: it was quite literally a bar in the sky. I flipped through some fashion and travel magazines laid out on a table as I munched on the lemon-infused almond-stuffed olives I ordered. I grabbed a handful of little wrapped dark chocolates from the bowl on the bar before heading back to my in-air office pod, musing about how this was very likely the peak of my life – and I was totally okay with that. I would have liked to have toasted myself with a glass of wine to celebrate, but didn't order one.

Many of the business trips I had done over the year were quite quick: I would fly in, have dinner, perform the contracted speaking engagement the next day, and leave either that night or the next morning. Any extra time I had in each city I would spend at a museum, park, or downtown core, and I would always look forward to falling asleep watching TV in the hotel. But in Australia, I arranged to stay for a bit longer after the conference, as I'd travelled so far. I attended a speaking event featuring Douglas Murray and Dr. Cornel West in Sydney, and went on Australian national television as a panelist on the ABC show Q&A. I can't say live televised panel discussions were my forte, as I wasn't great at inserting myself into conversations with multiple voices clamouring to be heard (especially when one of the panelists was Dr. Cornel West, a philosopher and scholar who had the type of demeanour that dominated a conversation).

Nevertheless, I liked the format of the show – the live audience asked questions directly of the panel, and social media discussion around the show was lively. I checked the Q&A Twitter hashtag after my appearance, and saw at least two comments about how I, a white woman, should have been replaced with an indigenous woman. Some of the other participants on the show were Anne Aly, an Australian MP, and Eric Abetz, a senator for Tasmania since before I was born. The show's format also included a People's Panellist, where any "regular joe" can apply to come on the show and sit alongside the politicians and other notable guests, which I thought was a brilliant concept. It was pretty cool that I was on a panel with some of the county's elected politicians: Canada's stale media landscape offered nothing like this, where our political class could be confronted by everyday people.

*

The defense of my MA paper, "Free Speech on Campus: A Snapshot of the Present," was scheduled shortly after my return from Australia.

I presented my paper, answered the questions asked of me, and paced out in the hallway as my supervisor, Prof. Sweedler, and second reader, Prof. Haskell, deliberated. When I was invited back in the room, they congratulated me: I passed. There was only one thing in my way from knowing whether I would successfully graduate or not: the harassment complaint.

Finally, in September, Dawn McDermott from the dispute resolution office emailed me and told me the investigator's report was ready.

Dawn handed me the hard copy of the report. I inhaled.

> *Based on a comprehensive review of all evidence related to the matter and on the balance of probabilities, the Investigator has found that you did not breach the University's Harassment Policy.*

> *Assessment of Evidence*

> *The Investigator found that the Complainant's allegations against the Respondent were unsubstantiated. This conclusion results from the following:*

> *The parties did not know each other and had no past history prior to the commencement of their graduate programs in September 2017. They had no interaction with one another until November 2017. In November 2017, Mr. Jackson became aware of Ms. Shepherd's political views which she regularly posted about on her Twitter account. Mr. Jackson was heavily involved in student politics, activism and support services (i.e. volunteer coordinator of the Rainbow Centre and involvement at the Centre for Women and Trans People). Mr. Jackson, as a trans individual, was both opposed to and offended by Ms. Shepherd's political stance.*

> *The issue, however, is that Ms. Shepherd did not post any negative or derogatory commentary about trans people. Rather, she posted many negative comments about the University and the Communication Studies department. She admitted that she posted a clip from Mr. Jackson's speech (at the Trans Solidarity Rally) and highlighted his remark that "violence is okay." On her Twitter account, Ms. Shepherd also called Mr. Jackson a "conspiracy theorist" and asked "aren't you the person who dressed up in a genitalia costume and effectively shut down a talk by an MP at UWaterloo?". Many*

of Ms. Shepherd's followers posted negative and defamatory commentary about Mr. Jackson based upon Ms. Shepherd's posts about him. There is no dispute that Ms. Shepherd brought negative online attention to Mr. Jackson and that some of those comments were related to his trans identity. However, Ms. Shepherd's comments were not related to Mr. Jackson's trans identity. She denied that she was accountable for her followers' posts and emphasized that negative comments are a part of being on social media and online.

Moreover, Mr. Jackson directly tweeted at Ms. Shepherd, thereby opening himself up to commentary from her Twitter followers. Mr. Jackson had a significant online presence and was quite vocal about his own views and in his political activism. He spoke at the Trans Solidarity Rally on December 7, 2017 and placed himself in the public sphere as he demanded accountability from the University for queer and transgendered people. Ms. Shepherd emphasized, and the evidence appears to corroborate, that she did not post anything about Mr. Jackson that was not publicly available. Several of her tweets responded directly to his and therefore Ms. Shepherd did not "dox" Mr. Jackson and reveal private and personal details about him.

Mr. Jackson admitted that he began to tweet at Ms. Shepherd because of her abhorrent politics that invalidated trans identities. He emphasized that she cultivated an environment in which anonymous users displayed hate and transphobic rhetoric. Mr. Jackson admitted that Ms. Shepherd was not the one who initiated the transphobic rhetoric but stated that "she didn't step in or talk about that or address it; she let it cultivate and planted the seed." The posts on Twitter are consistent with Mr. Jackson's statement that Ms. Shepherd did not "step in" and respond to any of the negative or defamatory posts about Mr. Jackson. The issue, however, is whether Ms. Shepherd's lack of interference amounted to harassment and/or discrimination.

The evidence establishes that the climate at the University, following the media coverage involving Ms. Shepherd, was extremely difficult for Mr. Jackson, as a trans individual. Ms. Shepherd's Twitter account includes hundreds of messages that were derogatory towards the trans community and tried to invalidate their existence. While it is reasonable for Mr. Jackson to infer that Ms. Shepherd held similar views against trans people, there is no direct commentary from her in that regard. It was in that climate, however, that Mr. Jackson felt unsafe as a trans individual. It is well-known that there is a high rate of violence against the trans community. Therefore, it is highly plausible that Mr. Jackson felt unsafe in Ms. Shepherd's presence given that he felt she had caused the transphobic rhetoric.

Mr. Jackson and Ms. Shepherd did not have any in-person interaction until January 17, 2018 when he saw her in the Communication Studies lab... Mr. Jackson felt intimidated and unsafe by Ms. Shepherd's presence in the lab because of the negative online commentary against him on her Twitter page, which from his perspective, Ms. Shepherd cultivated and supported. On the other hand, Ms. Shepherd provided a legitimate explanation for why she was in the lab and emphasized that she was a TA in Communication Studies and had every right to be in the lab. Ms. Shepherd admitted she called Mr. Jackson "petty and pathetic." While the comment was negative and unwelcome, it was not related to Mr Jackson's trans identity. Ms. Shepherd emphasized that the comment was in response to Mr. Jackson confronting her about not being in the lab when she was entitled to be there. She indicated that he continued to tell her that she should not be there even after she explained that the printer in the CAST lab was not working. The evidence establishes that the parties' interaction on January 17, 2018 was a mutual conflict or disagreement.

However, the parties' interaction on March 19, 2018 was more problematic. Both Ms. Shepherd and Mr. Jackson described a situation involving an event featuring Faith Goldy and the distribution of marketing materials that resulted in an unwelcome and difficult encounter. It is important to note that at the time of the incident Mr. Jackson had been feeling unsafe for several months on campus and in Ms. Shepherd's presence. It is highly plausible that the presence of two males with Ms. Shepherd in the Communication Studies hallway, while Mr. Jackson was alone, left him feeling uncomfortable. Ms. Shepherd and the two males were hanging up Faith Goldy posters, an organized event which greatly offended Mr. Jackson.

The evidence establishes that Mr. Jackson felt intimidated and unsafe by Ms. Shepherd and the two males on March 19, 2018 when she followed him with her phone and appeared to videotape him. On the other hand, Ms. Shepherd provided a reasonable explanation for her actions. She was upset that Mr. Jackson took down their posters and followed him so that they could hang them back up... Ms. Shepherd explained that she was concerned that Mr. Jackson might interfere with the event and she wanted photo evidence of his interference. [n.b. It did turn out that Ethan organized the protest against the LSOI event].[83] *She admitted that perhaps she should not have tried to take the photo but maintained that given Mr. Jackson's past history (saying "violence is ok") she felt justified in doing so.*

Mr. Jackson expressly denied that he took down any posters, except for one in the stairwell that said "White Lives Matter" so that it could be reported. He repeated more than once that he did not rip down any posters even though Ms. Shepherd mistakenly believed he did. Ms. Shepherd emphasized that Mr. Jackson took down several posters and that she observed him doing so. The evidence confirms Ms. Shepherd's recollection of the events as a witness observed Mr. Jackson removing "at least two, maybe three posters." This evidence lends credibility to Ms. Shepherd's version of events and perspective.

So there you have it. He had lied during his meeting with the investigator! I remember telling the investigator that I had unmistakably seen Ethan shove posters in his pocket after he ripped them down, and she had seemed very interested in that detail.

The report concluded, "it follows that the Respondent, on a balance of probabilities, did not breach the 'harassment' and/or 'discrimination' sections of the University's Harassment Policy. It is more likely than not the alleged conduct was based on a divergence of political views and 'an interpersonal conflict or disagreement' with Mr. Jackson, which is explicitly defined as an exception under the Policy."

I had confided in a few people about the complaint over the summer, and realized that anybody who's anybody has had a complaint filed against them. I now knew of at least a dozen professors and other working individuals who had had been accused of unprofessionalism, discrimination, subordinance, and even sexual assault. But the complaints were always ridiculous and overreaching – filed by people who were angry and vengeful.

When I heard from people who had been accused of sexual assault at work and had later been cleared, I realized I still had the lingering thought in my mind – well, what if there really was something to that complaint? Even when you're found in the clear, there is a stigma that comes with the fact that a complaint was made against you in the first place. But ultimately, I'd rather be around people who have had a complaint made about them than people who haven't. In our stifled culture, it was the sign of an edgy or interesting person.

With the complaint cleared, my coursework complete, and my MA paper successfully defended, that was that: I was going to graduate from Wilfrid Laurier University.

CHAPTER 19

In September, I started looking for work, as the plan was to stay in Waterloo until December, at which point Cosmin would finish his English degree at the University of Waterloo and we would move to British Columbia, my home province. A part of me wanted to keep living in Kitchener-Waterloo. I had arrived there thinking it was a generic place, with too many big box stores and a perpetually empty uptown plaza. But my first impression wasn't accurate: Waterloo was a lovely place.

I would miss bicycling up to St. Jacob's, and seeing the Mennonite horses and carriages clopper by. I would miss the local cafes I studied at every day over a mug of hot coffee and a lemon tart. I would even miss trudging through the snow at the Laurier campus in the winter.

Waterloo, Ontario was a special place to me now. But at the same time, I had grown uncomfortable living there. When I was recognized in public, it was principally in Waterloo, as my story had been covered in the local news extensively. At the height of the controversy, in November–December 2017, I was recognized at least once a day.

In the summer, I was studying at a cafe when I saw someone had tagged me in a tweet saying they had just seen me there. It was a neutral tweet – in no way aggressive or harassing – but I was put off. It was a feeling of being seen by people who knew about you when you didn't have that reciprocal knowledge of them.

In the spring, I was ordering a tomato soup and iced coffee at an eatery, and the cashier tilted her head at me and said, "You look familiar. Do you go to Laurier?"

"Yes, I do," I smiled, putting my debit card back in my wallet and taking my number to a table.

When she came to bring me my order, she said tersely, "I just realized who you are. I'm sorry."

She's "sorry?" I thought to myself, scratching my head. *What is that supposed to mean?*

I liked to drift through the places I lived in anonymously, which meant I would have to leave Waterloo, at least for now.

But to hold me over for the next couple months, until my departure, I found part-time work as a court reporter in Mississauga. My job was to sit in on legal discoveries and take notes. It was a two and a half hour commute from Waterloo to Mississauga, each way. At the time, it was quite miserable: I woke up just before 6:00am and had to be out my door in the dark chill of 6:20am to catch the bus, to arrive by 9:30am. I ate a quick bowl of cereal in the morning, and packed myself a large bottle of half-water half-orange juice for the commute. I was usually on the verge of throwing up the entire bus ride, and the only thing to quell my nausea was leaning my head back, closing my eyes, and slowly sipping the diluted juice over the next couple hours as we zoomed down the highway through Kitchener, Cambridge, and Milton. Why was I nauseous? Oh right, I forgot to mention: I was pregnant with my son, Basil.

My now-husband Cosmin and I went to Parry Sound for a weekend in October, where he proposed. We rented a lakeside cabin, and I was warming up near the fire while reading a book in the late afternoon when Cosmin called me over to the dock and told me he caught a fish. I ran over, and he handed me the rod.

"You reel it in! I want to get a picture of you catching the fish!" he said.

I started reeling, but didn't feel the weight of any fish.

"Are you sure there's a fish? I don't think –" I swiveled around to see Cosmin with a ring box in his hand.

215

"I was going to put it on the fishing rod, but I was too scared of losing it," he said.

*

At the end of October, I would be walking in my convocation ceremony and graduating with my MA.

But there were some loose ends to tie up. With my graduation and departure, we would be dissolving the Laurier Society for Open Inquiry. Most of the other executive members were either in their last semester or last year of school, and none of us were keen on trying to find a suitable successive club president when it seemed that the majority of students were not willing to undertake any endeavour that might be deemed controversial.

As a last hurrah, LSOI organized one final big speaking event: "Does Trans Activism Negatively Impact Women's Rights?", featuring feminist writer Meghan Murphy. An acquaintance from my graduate English class recommended I invite Murphy, as she was controversial in feminist circles. Murphy was stalwart in her position that trans women should stay out of women's shelters, prisons, washrooms, and changing rooms, and instead create their own trans-specific spaces, as male-bodied persons in female spaces pose a safety risk to women and girls. In the case of sports, some are willing to pretend male-born trans women can fairly compete against natal women and possess no biological advantages – but Murphy was not willing to go along with that narrative.

When we requested a room from Laurier, the school upped the ante from Dr. Widdowson's May talk, which had cost just over $5,000 in security fees – they quoted us $8,055 for the Murphy event. I sighed: here we go again.

We set up another fundraiser, but we didn't have enough time to raise such a large amount of money, as Laurier had only given us a couple days to hand over a cheque. When the deadline passed, I sent Meghan a defeated email:

> *It doesn't look great right now. Having the event at Laurier is now not an option. I was in contact with two municipal venues in the Waterloo region (the only ones that had space) but once I gave them the title of the event and mentioned we would be hiring our own security, email communication dropped off on their end.*

> *I'd be happy to talk on the phone about this, but I think the best course of action right now is for me to refund the tickets/GoFundMe, and cancel the event.*

> *Let me know whether you agree.*

> *Thanks and sorry about this mess.*

Meghan replied, urging me not to cancel. "We can't let 'them' win," she wrote. "This is what they want."

I breathed in. She was right. I opened my laptop and looked up any and all local Kitchener-Waterloo venues. I stumbled across a municipal hall, The Aud, which had a perfectly-sized room called the Wright Auto Sales Lounge (the name caused BC trans activist Morgane Oger to later falsely claim we had been relegated to holding the talk at a car dealership).[84] I called The Aud that day, less than an hour after receiving Meghan's email, and surprisingly, they gave me a yes, and they were very helpful in planning the event with me. I was grateful that Meghan hadn't allowed me to give up.

The Aud only charged us $1,500 in security fees, as opposed to the grossly inflated $8,055 figure posed by Laurier. As expected, activists and detractors were bragging on Twitter about ripping down our event promotion posters. They were also circulating the phone and extension number for the City of Kitchener event services line, saying "The event 'Does Trans Activism Negatively Impact Women's Rights' is hosted by an anti-indigenous & transphobic group from Laurier and features an anti-trans speaker... Contact the City of Kitchener to ask them to cancel the booking."

But in the end, the event happened successfully, and there were only a dozen or so masked protesters outside the venue, consisting of the usual suspects from the local Antifa group, as well as Toby from the Rainbow Centre.

Several days after the event, I was studying at the University of Waterloo with Cosmin, and grabbed a copy of the University of Waterloo school newspaper, the Imprint, at one of the stands. There was an article in the paper about an event titled "Love Letters to Inclusive Feminism," a crafting session organized by the Rainbow Centre to counter LSOI's Meghan Murphy event.

"Feminism is not only for women. It has grown to include equality for all genders, whatever they may be. Still, an air of transphobia persists in some radical feminist circles," the article read.[85]

"To counter the arrival of one such transphobic speaker on the Laurier Campus, the Rainbow Centre, the Laurier Students' Public Interest Research Group (LSPIRG), and the Centre for Women and Trans People held the Love Letters to Inclusive Feminism event on Wednesday, Oct 24th."

This article was participating in the curious trend where anyone disliked by the writer is never mentioned by name. Meghan Murphy's name was not mentioned: she is only identified as "one such transphobic speaker."

The Love Letters to Inclusive Feminism event "included relaxing recreational activities for attendees. Colouring pages were set up in the centre of lots of food and drinks, as well as resource pamphlets, self-care cards, and buttons."

I shook my head. Because LSOI was partaking in a critical discussion on a current societal issue, in a completely separate location on the other side of town, some other students needed colouring pages, elementary school-level crafts, and snack time to deal with the trauma. It was childish. It was shameful.

CHAPTER 20

Graduation day was here. I waited in the procession line with about half of my MA CAST classmates – the others hadn't completed their requirements on time. We did not exchange any greetings. While looking at my classmates, donned in graduation caps and regalia like I was, I felt eternally grateful for my experience at Laurier. I was grateful for my encounters with agenda-driven ideologue professors, grateful for the petty graduate students, and grateful for the spineless university administration. Because if I had been graduating like one of my colleagues right now, having completed a 12-month MA program in a department that taught me nothing, I would have been bitter for wasting a year of my life.

I could almost see how lost my classmates were when I looked at them: they had that slightly frightened look of "what do I do now?" But I had gotten a wake-up call. I was coming out of Wilfrid Laurier University equipped with a newfound sense of self: I had learned to trust my instincts. There were so many people still suspicious that I had planned everything all along throughout the Laurier controversy, and that I had mapped out a whole media strategy. But the boring truth was that I was propelled by instinct the whole way through.

I also learned that it was okay to articulate my thoughts without the backing of some leftist-approved academic theory. After half a decade as an arts student, I had internalized the notion that for any of my thoughts to be valid, they needed to be filtered through the lens of anti-capitalism, feminism, critical race theory, postmodernism, poststructuralism, or queer theory. But I no longer felt the need to rely on the crutch of one of the aforementioned theories to feel like my ideas were legitimate. Too often, postsecondary liberal arts education taught students that if you couldn't cite Foucault, Lacan, Derrida, Deleuze, Judith Butler, or Kimberlé Crenshaw, your arguments weren't worth anything.

I was also equipped with new insights into the state of academia, and our culture as a whole. I now knew that too many of the people lurking in university arts departments were not to be revered, and I now fully understood the perniciousness of the phrase "diversity, equity, and inclusion." I had also been confronted with the empty obscurantism of many humanities programs. I looked back on the website for the MA CAST program, the website I had looked at when I decided to apply to Laurier, and thought, how could I not have known? The list of course offerings had titles like:[86]

- CQ610: Race, Gender and Imperialism
- CQ613: Nostalgia and Exile: Memory, History and Identity
- CQ615: Theories of Multiculturalism and Intercultural Dialogue
- CQ618: Biopolitical Theory
- CQ621: The Social Body
- CQ624: Rethinking the Body via Deleuze and Guattari
- CQ625: Ethics, Affect and Embodiment
- CQ632: Hybrid Discourses, Discourses of Hybridity
- CQ633: Power, Hegemony and Resistance
- CQ640: Special Topics in Globalization, Identity and Social Movements
- CQ641: Special Topics in Body Politics
- CQ642: Special Topics in Culture and Representation

When I first applied to Laurier and saw these courses, I thought they sounded intriguing and exciting; now I knew how to read a course description and pick up on the indicators of political correctness and intellectual emptiness.

Above all, I had learned, during my year at Laurier, that far too many people simply do not believe in upholding the values of free expression and open inquiry on campus, and instead shamelessly advocate for conformity and censorship.

After walking across the convocation stage, back at the reception, my dad told me, "When you were walking across the stage, Deborah MacLatchy's eyes were following you the whole time."

"Oh, yeah? What expression did she have?" I asked.

"No expression really, she was just... looking."

*

Back in 2016, I had come across the story of the Graduate Students' Association firing the Veritas Café manager over his humorous job posting that incorporated the word "slave," and thought it was a one-off, that it was not indicative of any larger issue of political correctness or censorship.

I knew that future Laurier students who had followed my case would think the same thing to themselves: the Laurier affair was an unfortunate situation, perhaps, but not representative of a bigger picture.

Nathan Rambukkana and Herbert Pimlott quietly went back to teaching at Laurier, the semester right after my departure. Though they were both nowhere to be found for the entirety of 2018, they collected their full six-figure salaries that year: $104,887 for Rambukkana and $152,270 for Pimlott, plus benefits. They have both been awarded pay raises since then: Rambukkana made $109,852 in 2019, and Pimlott $160,207. Adria Joel got a new job as a coordinator with the local sexual assault support centre closely tied to Laurier.

Immediately after I graduated, the Diversity and Equity Office changed their name and rebranded to the Centre for Student Equity, Diversity and

Inclusion. They were granted increased funding from the federal government. They hired more staff.

As for me, I haven't completely lost my love of the university, and education is still among the values dearest to me. I have always envisioned myself popping back into university to take courses in languages, history, and science – education is a lifelong pursuit, not something you pursue in your youth and then never again. My intention with going to the media with my secret recording was to expose the suppression of free thought in academia so that the issue could be identified, understood, and rectified. But that did not happen at Laurier. Nothing had been rectified.

I got to meet Christie Blatchford, the journalist who first broke the story, in June 2019, when she was receiving the Justice Centre for Constitutional Freedoms' 2019 George Jonas award in Toronto.

During the Q&A session following her acceptance speech, in response to the question about the generational divide between old and young people defending individual liberties, Christie said, "I think all of us, when we're young, are stupid. Most people aren't Lindsay Shepherd, you know, at that age most of us are dopey... I don't remember being a particular defender of freedom when I was in my 20s, I was mostly at the pub."[87]

The audience laughed, and I smiled up at her.

It was the only time I would meet Christie Blatchford in person – I was fortunate to have gotten the chance to thank her for her work in person. She died of cancer in February 2020.

*

I have always been the type to make the best of any situation I found myself in, and I believe I did exactly that in the case of the Laurier controversy. But it is undeniable that there are consequences to publicly identifying yourself as someone who is not willing to go along with the ideological tenets of diversity and inclusion. Many job postings in academia, university management, the nonprofit sector, and the cultural industries specifically state they are searching for a candidate that lives by the principles of diversity and inclusion and will demonstrably uphold those principles. In early 2020, I was offered a sessional instructor position at a small college, to teach a course on media literacy the following year. A few days after showing my face at the online faculty orientation session, I was informed that a social justice-oriented faculty member figured out who I was, and my contract was swiftly cancelled.

Because I had involved the media in the Laurier affair since day one, there is no way to know what would have happened to me had I not gone that route. Without media and public pressure, I would have never found out that in reality, the "one or more complaints" facilitated by Rambukkana, Pimlott, and Joel didn't even really exist: I would have gone the rest of my life thinking that by taking a neutral stance on pronouns, I had deeply hurt and offended one or several of my students. If I had stayed quiet about this issue, and accepted the triad's claims at face value, who knows how I might be conducting myself or censoring myself for the rest of my life.

Yes, I faced some challenges at Wilfrid Laurier University, but I can only look back fondly on my year at graduate school in 2017–2018.

It was a time of momentum, energy, connection, liveliness, and fun.

AFTERWORD

When I first walked out of that fateful meeting with Rambukkana, Pimlott, and Joel in November 2017, I had been under the impression that nothing like the meeting I had just endured had ever happened before in a university.

I had thought that my case at Laurier was totally new territory. In some ways, it was. But I had stumbled right into what people were referring to as "the culture wars" – online debates and discussions about issues like political correctness, gender, feminism, trans activism, free speech, Trump, and the like. In my previous life, I went to class, went to work, went hiking, and studied French, Spanish, and Persian. I hadn't heard of the 2015 Yale screeching girl incident featuring Nicholas Christakis, or the 2017 Bret Weinstein controversy at Evergreen College, or the long list of incidents that happened in Canada, including at Laurier. In March 2017, for instance, Toronto lawyer Danielle Robitaille was supposed to deliver the keynote speech at the Laurier Criminology Student Association conference, but student outrage caused her to cancel over concern for her personal safety. Because Robitaille was a lawyer of former CBC radio host Jian Ghomeshi, who was tried and acquitted for sexual assault in 2014, a student group called Advocates for a Student Culture of Consent formed to "resist" Robitaille's talk, on the grounds that it would retraumatize sexual assault survivors.

Time and time again, incidents like the Laurier affair occur. They happened before, and they continue to happen after.

A University of Victoria adjunct professor, zoologist Dr. Susan Crockford, had been teaching at the university for 15 years before she was advised in May 2019 that her time as an adjunct professor had ended, as an internal committee had voted against the renewal of her status. Crockford, an accomplished scholar who specializes in animal bone identification and polar bears, had argued against contemporary climate change wisdom by stating that polar bears are not threatened with

225

extinction, and that their populations are in fact thriving. No reasons were provided for her non-renewal, leading Crockford to conclude her contract was terminated "in order to suppress views on polar bears and related climate change issues."[88] There was an earlier sign that the university was uncomfortable with Crockford's research. She had been part of the UVic Speakers Bureau for several years, delivering lectures to schools and community groups. One of her presentations was about the origins of domestic dogs, and the other was titled "Polar Bears: Outstanding Survivors of Climate Change." But in 2017, she was banned from the Speakers Bureau for not confirming she could properly "represent the university." Crockford told the Financial Post the revocation of her position was "an academic hanging without a trial, conducted behind closed doors."

Mark Hecht, an instructor at Mount Royal University's (MRU) Department of Earth and Environmental Sciences, published an op-ed in the Vancouver Sun in September 2019 titled "Ethnic diversity harms a country's social trust, economic well-being, argues professor." The article reviewed current research on the topic of social trust in multiethnic societies and posited that immigration policy ought to be based on norms of cultural compatibility and cohesion. After immediate backlash from politicians, activists, and journalists, the Vancouver Sun deleted the piece from their website. Some of Hecht's colleagues sent a letter to MRU President Tim Rahilly expressing that they were upset the university didn't publicly condemn Hecht's "blatantly Islamophobic and xenophobic" op-ed.[89] Though the university publicly affirmed Hecht's right to freedom of expression, the field school Hecht was set to lead in the Spring 2020 semester was cancelled for no apparent reason.[90]

In the fall of 2019, a socially conservative, pro-life Christian student named Garifalia Milousis was running uncontested for the Vice-President of Equity position with the University of Ottawa Common Law Student Society (CLSS). She was set to be acclaimed as the VP Equity: nominations had closed and no one else was approved as a candidate. Milousis was committed to fostering ideological diversity and had served on the executive team for a number of clubs, including one focusing on combatting sexual exploitation and modern-day slavery. She was also part of the university's Committee on the Prevention of Sexual Violence, and her undergraduate degree was in political science and women's studies.[91] However, some social justice-oriented students did some digging into Milousis' views on abortion, her past of speaking out against Bill C-16, and her membership with the Runnymede Society, a national law student group interested in "debating the ideals of constitutionalism, individual liberty and the Rule of Law." Suddenly the CLSS's Chief Electoral Officer announced she had received "complaints" from students that they hadn't received sufficient notice about the upcoming byelection, and the deadline for nominations was extended. While Milousis was previously the only approved candidate and was set to be acclaimed, there were now five candidates in the running. Milousis ended up losing the byelection.

In late 2019, the University of British Columbia Free Speech Club had booked a space at UBC Robson Square to host journalist Andy Ngo on January 29, 2020. Ngo was to speak on the topic of Antifa violence. The club paid a room booking deposit in November, but were informed in December their booking was rescinded – with no reason provided other than to protect "safety" and "security." The case is now before the courts.

In March 2020, University of Alberta professor of anthropology Kathleen Lowrey, who describes herself as a gender-critical feminist, learned that an unspecified number of informal complaints had been made against her by students claiming she has made the classroom learning environment "unsafe."[92] Lowrey, who was serving as the anthropology department's associate chair of undergraduate programs, was subsequently asked to resign from her role. Lowrey refused, and stated that if the University wanted to fire her from her position as chair, they could provide her with a letter laying out the reasons for her dismissal. She then received a letter from Dean of Arts Lesley Cormack, which informed her that "your appointment to the position of Associate Chair, Undergraduate Studies in the Department of Anthropology will conclude effective July 1, 2020.

You are unfortunately not able to be as effective in this administrative role as the Department and Faculty require, and it is not in the best interests of the students or the University for you to carry on." Cormack offered no concrete reasons as to why Lowrey was being dismissed. Neither Dean of Students André Costopoulos nor the UAlberta department of Equity, Diversity, and Inclusion and Human Resources Services will speak to the question of how many individuals complained about Lowrey and what the complaints alleged.[93]

In the 2019–2020 academic year, a University of Manitoba medical student and Coptic Christian named Rafael Zaki was expelled after the university received 18 anonymous student complaints about pro-life and pro-gun rights postings Zaki had made on Facebook. The complainants claimed Zaki's opinions made them feel "unsafe," and of course, Zaki was never permitted to see these complaints. In July 2020, the University Discipline Committee concluded Zaki's statements were "misogynistic and hostile to women," which had a "negative impact on the learning and work environment."[94] The matter is now before the courts.

This is only a small sampling of instances where free expression has been stifled on campus. There are many more such stories that never make it into the media. And yet, professors and university officials continue to deny that there is any suppression of free speech, free thought, or open inquiry on campus: they scoff at the idea that there is an issue.

Shannon Dea, the University of Waterloo professor who said I had "bad pedagogy" on The Agenda with Steve Paikin, wrote an article in University Affairs titled "My office door and the campus free speech crisis that never was." She argues that because she can freely post pro-LGBTQ rainbow stickers on her office door, there must be no problem with free speech on campus.[95] There are many other careerist academics wishing to establish themselves as the most superior, level-headed, rational thinkers on the issue of free speech, and they do that by conceding that academic freedom has been sometimes threatened over the years, but they otherwise routinely deny that there is an overarching problem. Because these professors are careerists who get off on being mentioned in the books and works of others, I will not say their names.

In 2018, when the Progressive Conservatives were elected in Ontario under Premier Doug Ford, one of Ford's first moves was to require every university in Ontario to implement a statement on free speech that solidified each institution's commitment to freedom of expression, academic freedom, and open inquiry. This statement had to be passed by January 1, 2019. If Ontarian universities violated the principles of free expression, their government funding would be threatened. This caused swift backlash by the leftist professoriate and bureaucracy, who claimed that the "free speech crisis" is being manufactured.

The Public Service Alliance of Canada released a statement reading, bluntly, "There is no free speech crisis on Ontario campuses. This is an ideological fiction advanced by the government to justify interference in the academic governance and autonomy of Ontario's universities and colleges."[96]

Creso Sá, director of the Centre for the Study of Canadian and International Higher Education and editor of the Canadian Journal of Higher Education wrote in a University Affairs op-ed, "Most with a working knowledge of higher education would agree that we are nowhere near a free speech crisis in colleges and universities... The few cases that make the newspapers are upsetting and illustrate poor judgement from students, faculty, and administrators."[97]

In 2019, eight months after the Ontario university free speech policies had been put in place, every university had to file an annual report of any issues or complaints filed under the free speech policy. Only one event was reported to be cancelled in 2019: the University of Toronto denied a space booking request from the Canadian Nationalist Party in January 2019 over "safety concerns."[98] Because there was only one cancellation out of the 40,000 events that happened on Ontario campuses, that was enough to convince some people that there is no freedom of speech issue on Canadian campuses. But first we must consider that the vast majority of these university events are banal functions that would never be subject to protest or controversy – think of BA program information sessions, resume writing workshops, faculty orientation luncheons, dentistry conferences, career fairs, or engineer networking dinners.

We must keep in mind that students are disincentivized from hosting any kind of controversial event: they don't want to be labelled as fascists or right-wing trolls, and they don't have thousands of dollars to spend on security fees just to host a non-mainstream speaker. Moreover, students are self-censorious: it is ingrained in them to not express controversial views on campus, as they could be subject to equity office complaints or alienation from their peers. The incoming cohorts of students are controversy-averse and afraid of reputational damage.

Yet in the Globe and Mail, James Turk, director of the Centre for Free Expression at Ryerson University, said that Ontario's free speech policy was a "bad joke."

"There isn't a fundamental free expression problem at Ontario universities," Prof. Turk said to the paper. "The HEQCO [Higher Education Quality Council of Ontario] report confirms that 40,000 events were held and there was one cancellation. My view is this was all part of Ford playing to a right-wing base, suggesting that the elites in these liberal institutions need to be reined in so they respect freedom of expression."

Similarly, higher education consultant Alex Usher said "Presumably, the Ford government will claim this as a success since *obviously* it was its free speech policy which created such a felicitous outcome. The likelier explanation, of course, is that *free speech was never an issue in the first place,* and we are going through all this rigamarole to satisfy a handful of right-wing trolls."[99]

But as Keith E. Whittington said in his 2018 book, Speak Freely: "Although some still deny that there is a significant threat to speech on campuses, that position requires an almost willful blindness to what has been happening on college campuses big and small."[100]

The cancellation of controversial events is not the only measure by which we can understand the suppression of free discussion and open inquiry, as it does not account for any self-censorship that stops students and faculty from organizing events in the first place. It can't account for our culture of conformity and aversion to controversy.

In Canada, one is considered a respectable member of society if they are conventional, deferential to authority, and do not cause offense. This is deeply ingrained within us. But we'd be best off if we loosened up a bit and gave ourselves more room to explore new ideas and say what we think. Moreover, our universities are too concerned with taking a "customer is always right" approach, and caving to every student demand in order to attract and sustain more tuition-payers. Once our post-secondary institutions cease this corporatized approach, elevate their academic standards, and shut down their diversity offices, they will once again be in the position to nurture the open society.

Appendix A

Laurier responds to recent media articles

Nov. 16, 2017

PRESIDENT'S MESSAGE TO THE LAURIER COMMUNITY

To the Laurier community,

Our university has been in the headlines this week. The situation at the heart of the news stories and social media commentary is complex.

As president and vice-chancellor, I have a broad responsibility to balance the many and often-competing demands that come into play in these circumstances.

Let me deal first with the personnel and privacy issues. As a responsible employer, we are obligated to abide by government regulations, human rights legislation and our own university policies. To this end, we need to gather the facts of the situation and assess them in a deliberate, fair and respectful manner. To do this, we are in the process of engaging an impartial third-party professional. Given the personnel and privacy issues involved, this process will be confidential.

Related, but separate, are the important principles so closely associated with the mission of any university. I am confident that those associated with Laurier believe strongly in upholding the important principles of academic freedom, diversity of opinion, critical thought, the civil debate of competing ideas, free speech, and freedom of expression. The real question, however, is how do we encourage and implement these fundamental ideals in a world that's more aware of the importance of inclusivity and yet, at the same time, is growing more polarized?

I am encouraged by the many people who have been moved by the events of the past week to share their points of view. These issues are clearly important to a great many people at Laurier and beyond.

I believe that as a university community we need to have more conversations about how academic expression happens throughout our institution. To be focused and constructive, these conversations should take place outside of the specific contexts that, for good reason, are often constrained by privacy legislation, employer regulations, and other legal requirements. Both rights and responsibilities have to be included in these conversations.

To this end, I will be striking a task force charged with a mandate to explore and consult on how we encourage and protect these important principles at Laurier. My goal is that we work together as a diverse community to build on the many best practices already underway here and share our made-at-Laurier solutions with ourselves and the wider community.

In the coming weeks I will be seeking input on how best to populate the task force and refine its mandate. I look forward to hearing from all of you as we work together to illuminate the many positive ways in which we live and implement these important values and principles at Laurier.

Sincerely,

Deborah MacLatchy, PhD

Wilfrid Laurier University

Appendix B

Open letter from Nathan Rambukkana to Lindsay Shepherd

Nov. 21, 2017

Dear Lindsay,

I wanted to write to apologize to you for how the meeting we had proceeded. While I was not able to do so earlier due to confidentiality concerns, including your privacy as a grad student, now that the audio of the meeting is public I can say more. While I still cannot discuss the student concerns raised about the tutorial, everything that has happened since the meeting has given me occasion to rethink not only my approach to discussing the concerns that day, but many of the things I said in our meeting as well.

First, I wanted to say that when I was made aware of the concerns, I was told that the proper procedure would be to have an informal meeting to discuss it. In the process of arranging this, others indicated they should attend as well. This is one of the facets of working at a university, that meetings can often become de-facto committees due to relevant stakeholders being pulled in. My main concerns were finding out why a lesson on writing skills had become a political discussion, and making sure harm didn't befall students. However, in not also prioritizing my mentorship role as the course director and your supervisor, I didn't do enough to try to support you in this meeting, which I deeply regret. I should have seen how meeting with a panel of three people would be an intimidating situation and not invite a productive discussion. Had I tried harder to create a situation more conducive to talking these issues through, things might have gone very differently, but alas I did not.

Second, this entire occasion, and hearing from so many with passionate views on this issue from across the political spectrum, has made me seriously rethink some of the positions I took in the meeting. I made the argument that first-year students, not studying this topic specifically, might not have the tool kit to unpack or process a controversial view such as Dr. Peterson's, saying that such material might be better reserved for upper-year or grad courses. While I still think that such material needs to be handled carefully, especially so as to not infringe on the rights of any of our students or make them feel unwelcome in the learning environment, I believe you are right that making a space for controversial or oppositional views is important, and even essential to a university. The trick is how to properly contextualize such material. One way might be through having readings, or a lecture on the subject before discussion, but you are correct that first-years should be eligible to engage with societal debates in this way. Perhaps instead of the route I took I should have added further discussion in lecture, or supplementary readings. But instead I tried to make a point about the need to contextualize difficult material, and drew on the example of playing a speech by Hitler to do it. This was, obviously, a poorly chosen example. I meant to use it to drive home a point about context by saying here was material that would definitely need to be contextualized rather than presented neutrally, and instead I implied that Dr. Peterson is like Hitler, which is untrue and was never my intention. While I disagree strongly with many of Dr. Peterson's academic positions and actions, the tired analogy does him a disservice and was the opposite of useful in our discussion.

Finally there is the question of teaching from a social justice perspective, which my course does attempt to do. I write elsewhere about reaching across the aisle to former alt-right figures as possible unexpected allies in the struggle to create a better more just society for all. But hearing all of the feedback from people and looking at the polarized response I am beginning to rethink so limited an approach. Maybe we ought to strive to reach across all of our multiple divisions to find points where we can discuss such issues, air multiple perspectives, and embrace the diversity of thought. And maybe I have to get out of an "us versus them" habit of thought to do this myself, and to think of the goal as more than simply advancing social justice, but social betterment and progress as a whole.

While I think that such a pedagogical approach must still work not to marginalize some students, I think the issues are too complex to leave as a binary with protection of students on one side and protection of speech on the other. We should be striving for both, which is why I look forward to participating in Dr. MacLatchy's task force looking into these issues at Laurier, and I hope perhaps you might consider doing the same so we could together work towards an even stronger institutional future.

I'm sorry this came to pass the way it did, and look forward to moving past this and continue working with you as my TA and perhaps in the future.

Yours sincerely,

Dr. Nathan Rambukkana

Appendix C

Letter from the Presidents: Your Voice and The Task Force

NOVEMBER 29, 2017

For Immediate Release

To undergraduate and graduate students of Wilfrid Laurier University,

Laurier has been the center of a contentious debate pertaining to academic freedom and freedom of expression. Now that the University has publicized the composition of the Task Force on Freedom of Expression, the student body has an opportunity to directly contribute to this important discussion. As Presidents of your Union and Association, and student representatives on the task force, we have a duty to listen to our membership and ensure your perspectives are heard.

We want to acknowledge that the events of last week, and the subsequent discourse associated with this topic, has caused harm for some Laurier students. The dominant narrative surrounding this story has too often discounted the lived experiences of transgender and non-binary students, and as a result, questioned their very existence.

The principles of academic dialogue and freedom of expression are integral components of university learning. While debate is a productive tool of learning, it requires proper contextualization and intentional facilitation by instructors and teaching assistants. In this environment students learn to think critically, understand the nuance of complicated topics, and listen to the perspectives of their classmates. Educational engagement with challenging material should not willfully incite hatred or violence.

Over the coming weeks and going into next semester, our goal is to facilitate sessions for students to ensure *all* voices are heard. We will then compile the feedback and articulate it to the committee to assist in the process of achieving their mandate.

Undergraduate students have the option to email any responses directly to sufeedback@wlu.ca

Graduate students have the option to email any responses directly to feedback@wlugsa.ca

This is a challenging time for many of us at Laurier but it is through this adversity, we can find our strength and can grow as a community.

Sincerely,

Kanwar Brar
President & CEO
Laurier Students' Union

Natalie Gleba, MBA
President & CEO
WLUGSA

Appendix D

An open letter from members of the Communication Studies
Department, Wilfrid Laurier University

December 18, 2017

An open letter to our academic colleagues:

We are writing in response to the ongoing situation involving teaching
assistant Lindsay Shepherd and our colleagues Drs. Nathan Rambukkana
and Herbert Pimlott in the Department of Communication Studies at
Wilfrid Laurier University. We are writing to share our perspective, clarify
some information, and support our departmental colleagues and students.

A meeting with Shepherd, who is a student in the Cultural Analysis and
Social Theory (CAST) MA program, and was assigned a Teaching
Assistantship in Communication Studies as part of her MA funding, was
secretly recorded and sent to the media by the TA. This act sparked
columns and op-eds that rushed to assess the meeting, generalizing from
this single event a diagnosis of our program, the University, and the state
of higher education in Canada. We welcome the widening range of
perspectives on this situation that are beginning to emerge in the public
sphere.

We recognize that the meeting was mishandled. We specifically
acknowledge the power imbalance in the meeting, as Dr. Rambukkana

acknowledged in his open letter to his TA. In future meetings, where serious matters pertaining to the conduct of TAs are under discussion, we acknowledge that students should be encouraged to bring someone representing them and their interests. We would support a graduate student initiative to unionize TAs, which could provide student-employees with a grievance process and other forms of support in cases such as this one.

As we understand it, Dr. Rambukkana did not operate unilaterally when he called a meeting with his TA. Rather, we believe, he acted in response to a disclosure made by one or more students to University offices set up to provide confidential student support. Upon being notified of this disclosure, Dr. Rambukkana — as course instructor — understood that he had a responsibility to act in line with University policies, including those laid out in the Gendered and Sexual Violence Policy.

Shepherd is a Master's student in the CAST program who was assigned a Teaching Assistantship in Communication Studies as part of her MA funding. Because the Communication Studies program is large, the program is sometimes assigned TAs from outside its own graduate program. The student in this case is one of 6 Teaching Assistants and 2 Instructional Assistants who are collectively responsible for 14 tutorials for 350 students registered in CS101 (Canadian Communication in Context). In the context of a large course like this it is necessary to strive for consistency across tutorials. When TAs work outside their home department, we see the need to work toward more integrated TA training. Plans to augment existing TA training need to consider the constraints of TA contract hours within which we operate.

While the "free speech" of a single individual has dominated discussion surrounding this situation, "academic freedom" is also a decisive term in this context. Dr. Rambukkana exercises academic freedom as a course supervisor by setting parameters for the multiple tutorials that supplement his lecture. It is within the scope of a supervising professor's academic freedom to have workplace meetings with TAs regarding how course material is taught. CS101 is a mandatory course for majors in Communication Studies, and it sets foundations for the rest of the program's undergraduate curriculum. CS101 tutorials largely operate as workshops that address writing, grammar, and research skills. We maintain that the use of materials that invite controversy into the classroom needs to be approached with pedagogical care and forethought.

Public debates about freedom of expression, while valuable, can have a silencing effect on the free speech of other members of the public. We uphold the rights of trans, non-binary, and queer folk to be addressed in our classrooms in ways that they define. Those in positions of authority in the classroom — faculty, instructors, teaching assistants — are not sitting equally around the table with students. Instead, they have a responsibility to foster an environment of mutual respect and critical thinking, one wherein students should never feel that either their grades or their well-being could be impacted because of their gender, sexuality, race, class, or any other facet of their identity. We appreciate that our University has mechanisms through which students who feel unsafe, unfairly treated, or who have experienced intolerance in the classroom or otherwise in their role as student can make appeals and find support and resources to help them. We also acknowledge that we can do a better job of making students aware of these mechanisms. We are always so grateful when students do approach campus offices designed for reporting problematic classroom situations, as their courage makes us do our jobs better. We thank you for coming forward: you are such valued members of our community.

Charges that our program shelters students from real-world issues or fosters classrooms inhospitable to discussing contentious issues from different vantage points seem to us simply preposterous. Courses taught by Drs. Rambukkana and Pimlott — and many other professors in our department and across the university — directly confront societal issues ranging from poverty to the global economy, sexuality, racism, and beyond. We reject efforts of those who have seized this episode as a strategic opportunity to disparage disciplines and scholars with commitments to improving social and economic equality within universities and in society at large. Likewise, commentators who characterize our students as millennial "snowflakes" not only insult our students but also paint a dramatically inaccurate representation of what happens in our classrooms, where students participate in facilitated, respectful, and rigorous critical and scholarly discussion regularly.

Commentary on this event in the press and social media has emboldened individuals who see themselves as noble defenders of free speech to intimidate our faculty and students — to the point that protective measures have been taken in an attempt to secure their safety. Against this politics of revenge, we acknowledge the moral imperative to support and protect our colleagues and students. We urge our colleagues at Laurier and beyond to monitor carefully how this event has been framed and taken up. We agree with Laurier's President that we live in an increasingly polarized world; understanding the forces and discontent driving this polarization, including how they are at play in this situation and with what consequences, is a collective task in which we all have a stake.

NOTES

[1] "Head of Ontario university cafe fired over jokey help-wanted ad seeking 'slave.'" (17 December 2016). The National Post.

[2] Michael Laurence, "Biopolitics and state regulation of human life." (28 April 2016). Oxford Bibliographies.

[3] Malhar Mali, "The woes of academia." (21 November 2016). Areo.

[4] Lester Faigley, Roger Graves, and Heather Graves, "The little Pearson handbook." (2018). 3rd Canadian edition. Pearson.

[5] Transcript written with assistance from https://pastebin.com/2k3jjGKJ

[6] "Laurier responds to National Post column." (November 2017). Wilfrid Laurier University.

[7] Luisa D'Amato, "WLU censures grad student for lesson that used TVO clip." (14 November 2017). The Record.

[8] David Millard Haskell, "Suppressing TVO video, stifling free speech, is making Wilfrid Laurier unsafe." (15 November 2017). The Star.

[9] "Laurier launches third-party investigation after TA plays clip of gender debate." (16 November 2017). The Canadian Press.

[10] https://twitter.com/ThinGrayLine01/status/933116256617508865

[11] https://twitter.com/AndrewLawton/status/932790264858492928

[12] Mohammad Akbar, "Alt-right's new hero on campus bullies Laurier into an apology." (29 November 2017). NOW Toronto.

[13] James Wilt, "Canadian media just created another alt-right superstar." (27 November 2017). Canadian Dimension.

[14] "Your letters: Laurier battle about human rights, not free speech." (25 November 2017). The Star.

[15] https://www.facebook.com/lspirg/videos/10159681662170010/

[16] Simona Chiose, "Free speech protest at Wilfrid Laurier University caps turbulent week." (24 November 2017). The Globe and Mail.

[17] Jay Rideout, "Its [sic] trans students and staff who deserve an apology from Wilfred Laurier University [sic]." (5 December 2017). NOW Toronto.

[18] Luisa D'Amato, "Trans students at Laurier ask, who's listening to us?" (24 November 2017). The Record.

[19] Aaron Hutchins, "What really happened at Wilfrid Laurier University: Inside Lindsay Shepherd's heroic, insulting, brave, destructive, possibly naïve fight for free speech." (11 December 2017). Maclean's.

[20] Aadita Chaudhury, "The WLU/Lindsay Shepherd controversy was never about free speech." (28 November 2017). Medium.

[21] Safina Husein, "The big debate on campus: New perspectives on the Laurier scandal." (29 November 2017). The Cord.

[22] Joseph Brean, "Counter-protests at Wilfrid Laurier University over freedom

of speech turn — well, one man was shouting." (25 November 2017). The National Post.

[23] Peggy Lam, "Rancour of free speech debate led gender-diverse people to feel unsafe, advocates say." (29 November 2017). CBC News.

[24] Laura Booth, "Petition calls for safety measures to support trans people at Laurier." (27 November 2017). The Record.

[25] https://www.change.org/p/greg-bird-wilfrid-laurier-university-faculty-open-letter

[26] https://www.facebook.com/WLURainbowCentre/posts/dear-laurier-communityin-the-face-of-recent-media-attention-we-feel-it-is-our-re/1628430573891091/

[27] Jonathan Rauch, "Kindly inquisitors: The new attacks on free thought." (1993). The University of Chicago Press.

[28] Luisa D'Amato, "It's a disservice to trans students to 'infantilize' them." (29 November 2017). The Record.

[29] "WLUFA statement on recent events at WLU." (12 December 2017). Wilfrid Laurier University Faculty Association.

[30] Faculty union claims they face 'violent speech and actions' daily, but won't specify – to protect members." (15 December 2017). The College Fix.

[31] Letters to the editor: Responding to controversy on campus. (29 November 2017). The Cord.

[32] http://www.sfu.ca/convocation/honorary-degrees/past_honorary_degrees/2017.html#coyote

[33] "Rick's Rant - University Censorship." (29 November 2017). Rick Mercer Report.

[34] https://www.tvo.org/transcript/2475627/freedom-of-expression-on-campus

[35] https://twitter.com/blacklikewho/status/935936856591622145

[36] "Academic freedom at Laurier." (30 November 2017). The Agenda with Steve Paikin.

[37] https://twitter.com/buridan/status/933771768376020993

[38] https://www.facebook.com/WLURainbowCentre/posts/1639781466089335

[39] https://twitter.com/NewWorldHominin/status/935145333947998208

[40] https://www.facebook.com/WLURainbowCentre/posts/1643935195673962

[41] Aimée Morrison, "Smart, clever, or wise?" (29 November 2017). Hook & Eye.

[42] https://soundcloud.com/jonathan-kay-305072641

[43] https://www.congres2018.ca/sites/default/files/sites/default/uploads/documents/congress_2018_-_mml_-_full_chronological_-_2018-05-08.pdf

[44] Alex Usher, "Has everybody lost their damn mind?" (27 November 2017). Higher Education Strategy Associates.

[45] Paul Adams, "Lindsay Shepherd just reminded us of what universities are

for." (22 November 2017). iPolitics.
[46] Johanna Weidner, "Trans community voices concerns at Laurier rally." (7 December 2017). The Record.
[47] https://twitter.com/ThinGrayLine01/status/1080279400497725441
[48] https://www.youtube.com/watch?v=punBxW02LkU
[49] https://twitter.com/NewWorldHominin/status/951944664436817920/photo/1
[50] https://www.youtube.com/watch?v=F4LMBC1vaV8
[51] http://archive.is/UmV2D
[52] "Wait, what just happened? Looking back on 2017." (22 December 2017). CBC Radio.
[53] https://www.cbc.ca/player/play/1118443587523
[54] https://twitter.com/blacklikewho/status/942768871877914625
[55] Brian Batchelor, "The crying white girl: Lindsay Shepherd, victimhood and white positionalities." (16 April 2018). Hot Mess: Nasty Feminisms in Performance.
[56] Uri Harris, "'White women tears'—Critical theory on Lindsay Shepherd." (9 December 2017). Quillette.
[57] Alan Li, "Attending a meeting at Laurier Society for Open Inquiry." (14 February 2018). The Cord.
[58] https://twitter.com/neilbalan/status/976071559172456448
[59] https://twitter.com/StudentsUPres/status/976176410720198656/photo/1
[60] Mari Uyehara, "The free speech grifters." (19 March 2018). GQ.
[61] Peggy Lam, "University talk featuring anti-immigration speaker Faith Goldy cancelled after fire alarm pulled." (21 March 2018). CBC News.
[62] Lindsay Shepherd, "Why I invited Faith Goldy to Laurier. (22 March 2018). Maclean's.
[63] https://kitchener.ctvnews.ca/video?clipId=1353116
[64] Laura Booth, "Laurier campus divided after alarm derails speaker." (21 March 2018). The Record.
[65] Laura Booth, "Lindsay Shepherd tries again: Kitchener Public Library booked for lecture on immigration." (5 April 2018). The Record.
[66] Jasmin Zine, "Transphobia, Islamophobia and the free speech alibi." (4 December 2017). The Conversation.
[67] Jasmin Zine, "The alt-right and the weaponization of free speech on campus." (2018). Academic Matters.
[68] Ron Grech, "Timmins student wins national essay contest." (29 May 2018). The Daily Press.
[69] "Statement on freedom of expression." (29 May 2018). Wilfrid Laurier University.
[70] Kurtis Rideout, "Task force holds town hall meeting to discuss draft statement of freedom of expression." (24 April 2018). The Cord.

[71] http://homepage.tinet.ie/~odyssey/Politics/Quotes/Steyn.html

[72] Frances Widdowson, "What's wrong with official indigenous territorial acknowledgements?" (September 2018). Society for Academic Freedom and Scholarship Newsletter.

[73] www.facebook.com/events/1974640209518316/

[74] https://ca.gofundme.com/f/help-lsoi-pay-excess-security-fees

[75] "WLUFA re-emphasizes support for Indigenous peoples." (9 May 2018). Wilfrid Laurier University Faculty Association.

[76] Safina Husein, "Indigenous ceremony and community protests held on campus in response to LSOI event." (10 May 2018). The Cord.

[77] Safina Husein, "Indigenous knowledge fund created at Laurier." (30 May 2018). The Cord.

[78] "Support for indigenization at Laurier." (May 2018). Wilfrid Laurier University Student Life.

[79] "Statement on Fightback's recent activities in KW." (11 May 2018). The Revolutionary Communist Party of Canada.

[80] https://mediasite.uoit.ca/Mediasite/Play/dfc5e4dbe1f44969ae11a0b1121f6ea41d

[81] "WLUFA statement regarding recent lawsuits." (25 June 2018). Wilfrid Laurier University Faculty Association.

[82] Luisa D'Amato, "Laura Mae Lindo joins Catherine Fife on the NDP benches." (8 June 2018). The Record.

[83] Laura Booth, "Goldy talk shut down by fire alarm after hundreds gather to protest." (21 March 2018). The Record.

[84] Morgane Oger, "Municipal institutions need to add an anti-discrimination clause to facility rental policies." (24 April 2019). MorganeOger.ca

[85] Victoria Gray, "Love letters to inclusive feminism." (31 October 2018). Imprint.

[86] https://www.wlu.ca/programs/arts/graduate/cultural-analysis-and-social-theory-ma/course-offerings.html

[87] https://www.youtube.com/watch?v=u_say2pUXbQ

[88] Donna Laframboise, "Was this zoologist punished for telling school kids politically incorrect facts about polar bears?" (16 October 2019). Financial Post.

[89] https://twitter.com/FrancesWiddows1/status/1203380755423846400

[90] http://www.safs.ca/issuescases/mount-royal-oped/MRU_letter_SAFS.pdf

[91] Christie Blatchford, "Culture wars rear head over conservative candidate in university election." (1 October 2019). The National Post.

[92] Carolyn Sale, "Academic freedom and perceptions of harm." (2 June 2020). Centre for Free Expression Blog.

[93] Lindsay Shepherd, "Gender-critical feminist professor removed from

service role for making students feel 'unsafe.'" (10 June 2020). True North.

94 Barbara Kay, "Medical student expelled for refusing to change his personal beliefs." (3 November 2020). The Post Millennial.

95 Shannon Dea, "My office door and the campus free speech crisis that never was." (14 December 2018). University Affairs.

96 "Statement on government-mandated free speech policies" (n.d.). Public Service Alliance of Canada Ontario Region.

97 Creso Sá, "The theatrics of the Ford government regarding free speech on campus." (6 September 2018). University Affairs.

98 Joe Friesen, "Only one event cancelled for safety concerns after Ontario postsecondary free-speech directive: assessment." (4 November 2019). The Globe and Mail.

99 https://myemail.constantcontact.com/One-Thought-to-Start-Your-Day--Big-News-on-Free-Speech.html?soid=1103080520043&aid=EOBAodnY_vg

100 Keith E. Whittington, "Speak freely: Why universities must defend free speech." (2018). Princeton University Press.

ABOUT THE AUTHOR

Lindsay Shepherd was born in Victoria, BC in 1994, and earned her BA (Hons.) Communication from Simon Fraser University ('17) and MA Cultural Analysis and Social Theory from Wilfrid Laurier University ('18). She has been published in the National Post, Ottawa Citizen, Maclean's, Epoch Times, and Quillette, and has appeared on the Rubin Report and Mark Steyn Show. She has testified in front of the House of Commons Standing Committee on Justice and Human Rights and was the recipient of the 2018 Harry Weldon Canadian Values Award and the 2018 Outstanding Graduate Student Award from Heterodox Academy. Currently, she holds fellowships with True North Centre for Public Policy and the Justice Centre for Constitutional Freedoms and resides in British Columbia's Fraser Valley with her husband and toddler.